AbleMUSE
A REVIEW OF POETRY, PROSE & ART

NUMBER 10 / WINTER 2010

inaugural print edition

www.ablemuse.com

Able Muse Press
publishing the new, the established

Now available from Able Muse Press:

Able Muse Anthology
Edited by Alexander Pepple
Foreword by Timothy Steele

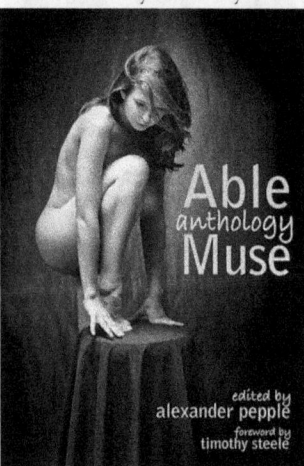

978-0-9865338-0-8 • $16.95

With R.S. Gwynn, Rhina P. Espaillat, Rachel Hadas, Mark Jarman, Timothy Murphy, Dick Davis, A.E. Stallings, Alan Sullivan, Deborah Warren, Diane Thiel, Leslie Monsour, Kevin Durkin, Turner Cassity, Kim Bridgford, Richard Moore and others.

". . . Here's a generous serving of the cream of Able Muse including not only formal verse but nonmetrical work that also displays careful craft, memorable fiction (seven remarkable stories), strking artwork and photography, and incisive prose." — X.J. Kennedy

Write Prize
for poetry & fiction

Deadline: February 15, 2011
$500 prize: poetry;
$500 prize: fiction

plus publication in Able Muse, Print Edition.
Final Judges: Rache Hadas (poetry);
Alan Cheuse (fiction)

Book Award
for poetry

Deadline: March 31, 2011
$1000 award

plus publication of winning manuscript by Able Muse Press.
Final Judge: Andrew Hudgins

Able Muse Review
~ Print Edition ~

Semi-Annual review of poetry, prose & art

Able Muse (Print) continues the excellence in poetry, art, fiction, essays, interviews and book reviews we've brought you all these years in the online edition. Subscribe at: www.ablemusepress.com

For complete details, visit: **www.AbleMusePress.com**

visit **online** for our more than a decade-old archives, plus web-only features not available in the print edition at:

www.ablemuse.com

Able Muse is not just another poetry site. It is one of the best sites on the Internet.
—Heather O'Neil, *Suite101.com*

A forum of Able Muse Review

Able Muse's premier online forums and workshop for metrical and non-metrical poetry, fiction, translations, art, nonfiction and discussions at:

http://eratosphere.ablemuse.com

Able Muse and its extraordinary companion website the *Eratosphere* have created a huge and influential virtual literary community. —Dana Gioia

Able Muse

www.ablemuse.com

Editor	Alexander Pepple
Associate Poetry Editor	Timothy Murphy
Nonfiction Editor	Gregory Dowling
Fiction Editor	Nina Schuyler
Assistant Fiction Editors	Tim Love, John Riley, Janice D. Soderling
Editorial Board	Rachel Hadas, X.J. Kennedy, A.E. Stallings, Timothy Steele, Deborah Warren

Able Muse is published semiannually. Subscription rates for individuals: $22.00 per year; libraries and institutions: $30 per year; single and previous issues: $14.95.
International subscription rate: $29 per year; single and previous issues: $17.95.
Subscribe online at www.ablemusepress.com or send a check payable to "*Able Muse Review*" to the snail mail address indicated below.

We read year-round and welcome previously unpublished manuscripts only. No simultaneous submissions. Online or email submissions ONLY. Submission guidelines available at: www.ablemuse.com/submit

Queries and other correspondence should be emailed to: editor@ablemuse.com
For paper correspondence, be sure to include a self-addressed, stamped envelope.

ISSN 1528-3798
ISBN 978-0-9865338-2-2

Attn: Alexander Pepple, Editor
Able Muse Review
467 Saratoga Avenue #602
San Jose, CA 95129

www.ablemuse.com
editor@ablemuse.com

Published by Able Muse Press: www.ablemusepress.com

Alexander Pepple

Editorial

Welcome to the inaugural issue of *Able Muse Review*, print edition. We hope to continue in this medium the more-than-a-decade-old tradition of excellence represented in the online archives at ablemuse.com, and in the recently released *Able Muse Anthology* (Able Muse Press, 2010). Thus, you will find in the print edition the same acclaimed standard of poetry, fiction, essays, book reviews, art and photography that has emblazoned the e-pages of the online edition.

This is a special-feature issue, which may not be obvious since it involves the editorial process used to choose most of the poems presented here. I produced a shortlist of fifty poems from about 4000 received during the submission cycle for this issue, then sought out the "guest editorial" opinion of five distinguished judges, and based on their most popular choices, derived what was eventually accepted. I would like to thank Timothy Steele, X.J. Kennedy, Deborah Warren, A.M. Juster, and Gregory Dowling for participating in this editorial special feature for the poetry section. Thus, we have some poems here I would not ordinarily include, and we are missing some that I would have personally chosen. Of course there were the most popular poems that almost everyone favored, myself included. One interesting fact was that none of the poems received a unanimous vote! I believe that this process resulted in a smaller number of accepted poems, but at a superlative standard, and minimal bias for the usual known names. At the end of it all, we have finely crafted poems from Catherine Tufariello, Catharine Savage Brosman, Leslie Monsour, Ned Balbo, Ted Mc Carthy, Gail White, Kim Bridgford, and others.

In this issue, we bring you—surprise!—R.P. Lister as featured poet. He was active up to 1980, publishing regularly in venues such as *Punch*, *The New Yorker*, *Atlantic Monthly*, and then, nothing more was seen from him. This is where Steve Bucknell's wonderful quest, documented at *Eratosphere* and in his memoir published in this issue, fills the gaps. There is also an interview with our 96-year-old featured poet by Steve Bucknell—yes, he is the oldest poet we have published, and indeed, one of the oldest published anywhere. I want to take this opportunity to thank Janice D. Soderling, our new assistant fiction editor, who crossed the genre aisle with the suggestion of featuring him.

We set a double record for contributor ages in this issue. At one end of the spectrum, there is our featured poet—the oldest we have published. At the other end we have accomplished fiction from Emily Cutler, a junior at Indian Springs School—the youngest we have published. There is also a gripping flash fiction from Nancy Lou Canyon and Marge Lurie returns with another wonderful story.

I am pleased to introduce our new fiction editor, Nina Schuyler, who replaces Thaisa Frank. We are grateful to Thaisa for all that she has done for *Able Muse* fiction and wish her much success promoting her new book, *Heidegger's Glasses* (Counterpoint, 2010). Our thanks also go to our assistant fiction editors, Tim Love, John Riley and Janice D. Soderling.

Not to be missed in this inaugural issue is a generous spread of riveting artwork from our featured artist Massimo Sbreni from Italy. Gregory Dowling, our nonfiction editor, brings us a compelling collection of essays on translation and scansion from Peter Filkins, Stephen Collington and Marilyn L. Taylor. Book reviews from Julie Stoner and John Whitworth complete our nonfiction section.

Finally, I want to welcome the new *Able Muse* advisory board members: Rachel Hadas, X.J. Kennedy, Timothy Steele, A.E. Stallings, and Deborah Warren. Their guidance will be invaluable with this new and exciting chapter of *Able Muse*.

Thank you for joining us in this special inaugural event—the *Able Muse*, print edition.

The very best,

Alexander Pepple
—Editor

CONTENTS

Alexander Pepple
   Editorial / *v*

ESSAYS

Peter Filkins
   The 'Other' Muse / *6*

Stephen Collington
   The Anyone-Can-Do-It Method for Writing Chinese Poetry (in Japanese)
   Thoughts on Language, Authenticity and Form / *16*

Marilyn L. Taylor
   Semi-Formal Verse and Its Prosody / *36*

MEMOIRS

Steve Bucknell
   The Mystery of R.P. Lister / *70*

FEATURED POET

Richard Percival Lister
   Interviewed by Steve Bucknell / *81*

POEMS

   The Length of Time / *85*
   Darling Death / *86*
   The Haunted / *87*
   Infected Eyes / *88*
   Stardust / *89*
   The Slow Loris / *90*
   The Stork / *91*
   Nokia / *92*
   To Be Alive / *93*

FEATURED ARTIST

Massimo Sbreni
    A Photographic Exhibit / *49*

FICTION

Nancy Lou Canyon
    A Terrible Storm / *1*

Emily Cutler
    Relativity / *108*

Marge Lurie
    Heat Wave / *141*

POETRY

Heather Hallberg Yanda
    It Will Never Be Beautiful / *3*

Peter Austin
    His Own / *4*

Trina L. Drotar
    In My Pocket / *5*

Gilbert Wesley Purdy
    The Quonset Hut / *32*

Jamie Iredell
    The Slot Tech / *33*

Maryann Corbett
    A Cautionary Tale / *34*

Steven Winn
    Postres / *44*

Ted Mc Carthy
    Nearly / *45*

Rebecca Foust
    The Speaker Tries Medication / *46*

David Alpaugh
    Richard Cory (His Untold Story) / *47*

Gail White
    A Crisis in Mesa Verde / *94*

J. Patrick Lewis
    At the Hotel Ukrainya A Century Ago / *96*

Frank Osen
    Ligan / *97*

Wendy Videlock
DEBRIEF / *98*
DEAR MOON, / *100*
IN BETH'S GARDEN / *101*

Ned Balbo
MARCO POLO COLLECTS BIRD EGGS / *102*

Leslie Monsour
IN SUCH A PLACE / *103*

John Beaton
TO THE DEAD OF WINTER / *104*

Catherine Tufariello
THE CRICKET IN THE SUMP / *106*

Kevin Corbett
NATURE / *107*

Catherine Chandler
DELINEATIONS / *134*
FLAMMARION WOODCUT PILGRIM REDUX / *135*

Susan McLean
MOONBURNED / *136*

Richard Meyer
COMMUNION / *137*

John Slater
FALLING ASLEEP / *138*

Kim Bridgford
BILLY WILDER'S GRAVE / *139*

Diane Seuss
WHAT'S BENEATH THE SURFACE OF THE SONNET? / *140*

Catharine Savage Brosman
ON THE MESA TOP / *148*
ARS POETICA / *150*

BOOK REVIEWS

Julie Stoner
MAXINE KUMIN, *WHERE I LIVE: NEW & SELECTED POEMS 1990-2010* / *119*
CARRIE JERRELL, *AFTER THE REVIVAL* / *119*

John Whitworth
JEFF CHAUCER, *A GARDEN OF ERSES: LIMERICKS* INTRODUCED BY ROBERT CONQUEST / *130*

CONTRIBUTORS' NOTES / *155*

INDEX / *161*

Able Muse Anthology

978-0-9865338-0-8 • $16.95

Edited by Alexander Pepple • *Foreword by* Timothy Steele

PRAISE FOR THE *ABLE MUSE ANTHOLOGY*:

This book fills an important gap in understanding what is really happening in early twenty-first century American poetry. **–Dana Gioia**

You hold in your hands a remarkable anthology of poems, translations, an interview, essays, short stories and visual art. **–David Mason**

This extraordinarily rich collection of fiction, poetry, essays and art by so many gifted enablers of the Muse is both a present satisfaction and a promise of future performance. **–Charles Martin**

Neither unskilled, lethargic, nor distracted from their proper enterprise, the muses in the past decade have been singularly able, as this outstanding anthology from *Able Muse* demonstrates. **–Catharine Savage-Brosman**

Here's a generous serving of the cream of *Able Muse*, including not only formal verse but nonmetrical work that also displays careful craft, memorable fiction (seven remarkable stories), striking artwork and photography, and incisive critical prose. **–X. J. Kennedy**

Mark Jarman, Rachel Hadas, Turner Cassity, Stephen Edgar, Timothy Steele, R. S. Gwynn, Rhina P. Espaillat, A. M. Juster, Geoffrey Brock, Annie Finch, X. J. Kennedy, Timothy Murphy, Jennifer Reeser, Beth Houston, Dick Davis, A. E. Stallings, Richard Moore, Chelsea Rathburn, David Stephenson, Julie Kane, Alan Sullivan, Kim Bridgford, Deborah Warren, Diane Thiel, Richard Wakefield, Rose Kelleher, Leslie Monsour, Lyn Lifshin, Amit Majmudar, Len Krisak, Marilyn L. Taylor, Dolores Hayden, Suzanne J. Doyle, Dennis Must, Thaisa Frank, Nina Schuyler, Misha Gordin, Solitaire Miles, and others.

---

from **Able Muse Press**

More information at: www.ablemusepress.com
Order at: **Amazon.com, BN.com, . . .**
& other popular online & offline bookstores

FICTION

Nancy Lou Canyon
A Terrible Storm

Lightnin rode the fence, jumped me while fixin barbwire, and you imagine cows leaning into the next pasture, reaching past camas as the electric bolt drills the cowboy, his cells popping like water on a hot woodstove, and, it's a miracle he's now sitting at the picnic table in the lookout tower, wearing dirty cowboy boots and blue jeans, a faded plaid shirt sporting mother-of-pearl buttons, and a stained hat he periodically removes, draws a skinny hand over thinning hair and replaces again, saying, *Doc packed me in ice to reduce the swelling,*

and you imagine him laid out in a waxed box that recently held a side of beef, and the butcher crossing the street, carrying that box from the market, emptied of raw beef he's just finished salting and seasoning—fifty pounds of prime rib to dry on racks, reducing to ten pounds of jerky that would soon sit in a smudged jar on a polished counter, and the bartender wishing for a twisted piece just as he gets the call—*Doc needs several wheelbarrows full of ice down at the clinic, pronto,*

and the cowboy leans into his wife and says, *Doc's young but pretty smart,* and she nods,

and you nod too, for the doctor found the mass in your abdomen not long after the miscarriage, reassuring you that it *probably* wasn't cancer since you were only twenty,

and the cowboy says his wife is a nurse, and she was waiting in the truck when it happened, and *Bein the strong woman that she is, she picked me up and slammed me on the ground over and over again, cause my heart stopped. Slammin starts it again,*

and you imagine his wife slamming him to the ground over and over again, next to the fence-line where the come-along held the post straight-up, defining his parcel of land on a prairie where storms pounded the earth like military raids, kicking up dust and rabbits, people too—some ducking into pickups, others hiding beneath store awnings, or swinging into taverns,

and you recall your own heart nearly stopping when a week earlier the lightning bolt hit the lookout tower, where you sat, looking for forest fires, the lightning blasting through the rod up top, flashing forty feet down into the ground below, and really, it's that kind of moment that makes you realize the significance of things being in good repair—the rod tightened down nicely, fittings shiny as copper pennies—and you feel safe knowing glass insulators cup all the chair legs in the tower, including the bench where the cowboy sits, legs stretched lankily, mouth drawn sideways, *What Doc did, and my wife,* the cowboy says, *all Goddamned miracles,*

and you say, *Yeah,* and, *You're lucky to be alive.*

And you wonder if the cowboy is one of those people who believes in prayer, like the woman in the paperback you'd been reading between watches, and it comes to mind how the heroine in that book had wandered into the back mountains to help the sick, praying for the dying, holding a feverish hand, never pleading for a life to be spared, just asking for His will to be done, and you wonder as you continue to observe the cowboy sitting there by his wife at the picnic table sprinkled with crumbs of Rye Crisp, as you touch your belly, if you'll be spared too.

Heather Hallberg Yanda

It Will Never Be Beautiful

It will never be beautiful—the scar's
grim mouth sewn silent. I'm certain even
the mirror has grown weary of it, part
knife-wound, part miracle. I imagine
the surgeons as they work: how intimate
their actions, tending the unforgiving
skin, honoring the body's resilient
structure, its universe within—cutting
apart what must be made whole. No suture
promises certainty, but the surgeons
understand just how capricious nature
is, see the singleness of each moment,
see how time, not hope, is truly fragile—
how the scar will always be beautiful.

Peter Austin

His Own

—Inspired by a short story by Zsuzsi Gartner

She sewed a brace of buttons on his shirt,
Conquered the smelly sweat stains using Lux
And, while it hung to dry, attacked his tux.

Scrubbing with soap and water cleansed the dirt
(Splotches of clotted ketchup on the vest);
The pants he wouldn't wear till they'd been pressed.

She trimmed his tache, his sideburns and his hair,
Repeating to herself her mom's advice:
You want to keep a beefcake, treat him nice,

Then, overcome afresh by how unfair
What she'd agreed to do was, asked again:
"Why wasn't I invited?" (a refrain

That sickened her but wouldn't stay unsaid).
"I told you twenty times: it ain't my call;
It's me alone or nobody at all;

"Now, help me tie this bow and bag your head." . . .
She learned—a good deal later and by phone—
The wedding that he'd gone to was his own.

Trina L. Drotar

In My Pocket

is a lipstick in the shade you
always said was too bold for me.

I wore Hot Buttered Rum
every single day that you
were not around. I kissed
envelopes, the back of my hand,
and that man down the street
whose name I no longer recall.

I bought ten, no twelve, and kept
one in each purse, two in the bathroom
drawer, the one on the upper left that you
never opened, and one in the freezer where
you'd never have thought to look. It was
always in between last week's leftovers and
some heat-and-serve cardboard dinner that you
always wanted.

ESSAY

Peter Filkins
The 'Other' Muse

Rilke's "Archaic Torso of Apollo" ends with a line that, despite its simplicity, is notoriously difficult to translate. "Du mußt dein Leben ändern," says the speaker, "You must change your life." Part of the reason why it's hard to convey all that is packed into this simple sentence is that it arises out of nowhere. Here is the poem in Stephen Cohn's translation:

> We never knew his legendary head
> nor saw the eyes set there like apples ripening.
> But the bright torso, as a lamp turned low
> still shines, still sees. For how else could the hard
>
> contour of his breast so blind you? How could
> a smile start in the turning thighs and settle
> on the parts which made his progeny?
> This marble otherwise would stand defaced
>
> beneath the shoulders, and their lucid fall;
> and would not take the light
> like panther-skin; and would not radiate
>
> and not break from all its surfaces
> as does a star. There is no part of him
> that does not see you. You must change your life.

The genius of the poem lies in Rilke's ability to assert what is not there by describing what is. We are told of what we cannot know or see by being convinced of its residue in what we do see. Thus, though the head with its "eyes set there like ripening apples" has disappeared, it "still shines, still sees." Otherwise, Rilke argues, the torso would not "take the light/ like panther-skin," nor "break from all its surfaces/ as does a star." It is the god who bursts forth, such that "There is no part of him/ that does not see you." In imagining the absent Apollo, the poet suddenly is stricken by his own inadequacy and need to "change." Or perhaps the voice of the god speaks the last sentence, admonishing the speaker to "change" his life. Another reading would argue this is Rilke's advice to the reader, the poet having introduced us to the power of the divine through his poem, reminding us of its sway within our lives and the important work of capturing it as artist, poet, viewer, or reader.

What the poem does not make clear, however, is exactly how we or Rilke are meant to "ändern" (pronounced with the "a" of "and") or "change." This, of course, is essential to the poem's uncanny mystique. How petty the command would seem if all it were telling us were to live a "better" life, to simply work harder, or to be a nicer person. Instead, the poem asks that we "change" our life, but without saying why or how. Meanwhile, the root of "ändern" in German is "ander" (pronounced with the "a" of "another"), which depending on the context, means "another" or "other" or "different," rather than "change." The definition of the verb "ändern" is "anders machen," which literally means to alter or make into something different. Hence, "You must change your life" doesn't quite capture the etymological nuance at work in "Du mußt dein Leben ändern." Better would be "You must make your life different," though that sounds awkward in English, whereas "You must live a different life" sounds more like a 12-step program than a spiritual watershed. "You must alter your life" would be another possibility, though it sounds like advice for a fitting, while "You must change the life you are living" has the ring of a doctor wagging his finger over your cholesterol chart. No, closer to the sea change Rilke intends here is what Käte Hamburger writes in *Rilke: An Introduction*: "[N]ow, in the face of the unexampled liveness of this statue, mere inspection would no longer be the adequate and appropriate response. The need to be equal to this, to meet the claim this work of art makes on the viewer—"for there is no place that does not see you"—breeds the desire to turn into a different person oneself; in what way and what direction remains open, unless one wishes to appoint the ever more intensively cultivated capacity for the viewing itself as the task of a lifetime."* There, that's the gist of it. Too bad it's a few too many syllables.

---

*   Quoted and translated by Walter Arndt as a footnote to his translation of Rilke's "Archaic Torso of Apollo," which appears in Arndt's *The Best of Rilke* (UP of New England, 1989). Interesting to note here is that Arndt also follows the more standard translation of the penultimate sentence or phrase by rendering it as "for there is no place [or part of the statue] that does not see you," rather than referring to "no part of him," or the god, as does Cohn.

My point here is not about the limitations or impossibility of translation, nor do I wish to review the various solutions for this line that translators have come up with over the last century. Cohn's is a fine translation, as are others, and his is the generally agreed upon solution for the poem's last sentence. Rather, I begin with Rilke's "Archaic Torso of Apollo" and its oracular ending in order to explore the possibilities of translation as an art form, as well as to examine the value of translation as a tool for aspiring writers in shaping their own craft. Through translation, and by considering the various layers of meaning at work in a statement as seemingly direct as "Du mußt dein Leben ändern," we come to realize the moment of poetry that Rilke wishes to resonate within us. Put differently, in realizing what the translation does not say or cannot say we appreciate what it is *trying* to say. This, too, corresponds to the action at work in Rilke's poem. As Cyrus Hamlin points out in an introduction to Walter Arndt's *The Best of Rilke*, "Absence for vision thus becomes presence for the imagination through the mediating powers of poetic language," in the "Archaic Torso of Apollo." Later, Hamlin links this to the act of translation when he states, "A translation [of this sonnet] . . . ought ideally to include a device like quotation marks around its own verbal performance to indicate that this text stands in relation to the original poem in a manner exactly parallel to the relation of Rilke's text to the hypothetical original statue of the god." That is, just as Rilke's poem conjures a god, so any translation must conjure the original poem. If the operation succeeds, then the god or true poem steps forth asking us to "change" our lives in the way that only great art, or a god, can do.

One might be quick to respond that access to such revelation depends on a fairly thorough knowledge of German, making this an insight limited to close scrutiny of the original. In this particular example, this is correct, though I'd counter that the linguistic skills needed to get what Rilke is after are not that advanced. More importantly, I'd also argue that the interpretive moment that opens up here is no different than that available to us in any great poem in English, and that rather than translation being a different skill or art form from writing or reading, it is only a more highly concentrated form of both.

Consider, for instance, Keats' famous trope at the end of "Ode on a Grecian Urn." While its closing lines, "Beauty is truth, truth beauty,—that is all/ Ye know on earth, and all ye need to know," may seem immediately comprehensible in their directness, even T.S. Eliot felt it impossible to know exactly what Keats meant by them. Add to this the textual variation which places quotation marks around "Beauty is truth, truth beauty," and even more confusion arises. Would this mean that the statement alone is made by the urn and the rest is Keats, or are the entire last two lines of the poem spoken by the urn, thus leaving Keats as puzzled as the rest of us? Either way the moment of revelation that passes between the inanimate and the animate here is quite akin to that which occurs in Rilke's poem. Each requires an interpretive leap on our part, one that keeps one foot in what is being said in the poem itself, while the other foot steps into what lies behind what is said. In this manner we as readers have to "another" our interpretive reading, or at least to alter our comprehension just enough to comprehend both what we know to be spoken and unspoken in the same line. It is this kind of "difference" that translation both explores and tries to solve, and there is much to be learned from such practice by any student of writing or literature.

One of the assignments I hand out early on in a translation workshop is a photocopy of the first page of four different prose texts: Welty's "Why I Live at the P.O.," Hemingway's "Big Two-Hearted River: Part I," James' *Portrait of a Lady*, and Woolf's *To the Lighthouse*. I then ask them to read each opening page and write about what would be difficult to render if they were translating the work into a foreign language. They quickly see the cultural barriers that exist in the Welty, whether it be the reference to Stella-Rondo's "Add-a-Pearl necklace," or the wonderfully native grammar of a sentence like "Mama said she like to made her drop dead for a second." Somewhat laughable are the possibilities we imagine for depicting the narrator having to "stretch two chickens over five people" for dinner. Equally ungraspable is Woolf's elongated syntax, the loops and dives of the consciousness at work in the piled-up phrases and clauses. James' lauding of "the ceremony known as afternoon tea" would also seem to pose problems if transferred to Swahili or Urdu, just as the seemingly innocent description of the "implements of the little feast . . . disposed upon the lawn of an old English country-house" is steeped in ideas of culture and class inseparable from the words themselves.

However, when we take a look at Hemingway's opening paragraph some surprising difficulties are revealed despite the seeming directness of the diction. Here it is in full:

> The train went on up the track out of sight, around one of the hills of burnt timber. Nick sat down on the bundle of canvas and bedding the baggage man had pitched out of the door of the baggage car. There was no town, nothing but the rails and the burned-over country. The thirteen saloons that had lined the one street of Seney had not left a trace. The foundations of the Mansion House hotel stuck up above the ground. The stone was chipped and split by the fire. It was all that was left of the town of Seney. Even the surface had been burned off the ground.

On first glance, the language would seem much easier to translate than Welty, James, or Woolf. Trains, baggage, towns, hotels, hills, and fire exist in some shape or form in every corner of the planet, nor are there any particularly dense phrases or erudite words in the passage. But the more that students look at the words and references, the harder it would seem to convey all that they actually describe. Why, for instance, is the landscape burned over, or what does it mean that Nick has purposely come to this place and yet betrays no hint of surprise at its condition? What kind of cultural roots lie entangled in the foundation of the "Mansion House" hotel, or what would be lost in merely duplicating the name "Seney" in another tongue without being able to strap to it the echoes of words like "seen," "scene," or perhaps even "sanity" or "sanitize"? And what about the sounds of that second sentence? "Nick sat *d*own on the *bund*le of canvas and *bedd*ing the *b*aggage man ha*d p*itche*d* out the *d*oor of the *b*aggage car." Is it possible that at the very same moment Nick is introduced into the story we also hear the rumble of bombardment on the front lines of World War I that Nick is trying to escape from? Is he in a way born out of the landscape of "*b*urnt tim*b*er" that ends the previous sentence? Finally, given all of this, or in the face of having to let go of some of it through translation, how would one convey the spiritual desolation of that last sentence? Indeed, though "the surface had been burned off the ground," it is the consciousness that makes note of it that is most at peril here.

My sense is that when students look at such a passage and how specific words create complex and ineffable effects, they stop reading what they have heard is a famous work of fiction and begin to engage with a marvelous and evocative work of literature. By the time they move from Nick's desolation in the first paragraph to his stark reassurance that "The river was there" in the second, and finally to his appreciation of the river's "surface pushing and swelling smooth against the resistance of the log-driven piles of the bridge" in the third, they find themselves in the hands of a master who has quietly taken them from the *b* of bombardment to the regenerative *s* of the sensuous in a single page. This of course is the arc of the entire story, and there's even the lovely accident of the printed edition moving from the mechanistic conveyance of "The train" that opens the first paragraph to the more natural flow of "the current" that closes the third paragraph at the bottom of the page. Such is the happenstance of art, though also what can drive the translator mad.

In that madness, however, lies much sense. In his essay, "Literature and Literalness," Octavio Paz states, "Translation and creation are twin operations." He goes on to remind us of the importance of translation in the development of any literature. What would Modern poetry be without the influence of Laforgue on Eliot? Think also of the importance of Vallejo, Lorca, and Neruda to Merwin, Wright, and Bly. The ascendant effect of Paul Celan's poetry on recent American poetry also cannot be ignored. Paz, however, also rightly points out, "Styles are collective and make their way from one language to another; works, all of them rooted in their own verbal soil, are unique. Unique but not isolated: each of them is born and lives in contact with other works in different languages. Thus neither the plurality of languages nor the uniqueness of works means an irreducible heterogeneity or an irremediable confusion, but the contrary: a world of relations made of contradictions and correspondences, unions and separations." Thus, all of literature is infused with translation. The Spanish poet influences the English poet who has been influenced by the

Provençal poet who shows up in the American poet, and so on. To this end, translation is the Research & Development wing of Literature. Without it there would be little at all that is genuinely new.

The fecundity of translation as a source for the making of literature also applies as much to the individual writer as it does to different cultures or literatures. As Paz wisely states earlier in the same essay, "Translation is a task in which, leaving aside the indispensable store of linguistic knowledge needed, the decisive factor is the initiative of the translator." This is why, he argues, "Translation involves a transformation of the original." If, however, we momentarily dispense with "the indispensable store of linguistic knowledge needed" to translate from one language to another, writing can also be seen as a process of translating literal experience into something called "literature," something that the novice writer must learn is central to what good writing actually does.

Teachers of writing everywhere have had the experience of students who will defend a piece of writing that may seem flat or uninteresting by saying, "But that's what actually happened." My response to this is often to remind them that one should never spoil a good story with the truth. Meanwhile, the mirror image to the student who will not let go of the original experience is the student who responds "That's just the way it feels" when asked about a poem or passage that is particularly obscure. In both cases the student is unwilling to take responsibility for his or her role as creator. In the first case it's the mystique of the "genuine" that prevents the student from seeing that what "really" happened was seen from one particular vantage at one particular time, and if it were rendered by anyone else who shared the same event or moment, it would most likely be described quite differently. On the other hand, the student unwilling to let go of the "original" expression, no matter how vague or ineffective it may be, thus foregoes the power of transformation inherent to the act of writing, that which alters the original experience in order to reveal its deepest truths, as well as revises the expression of that experience in order to share those truths more directly and compellingly with the reader.

Both of these students can benefit from thinking of themselves as translators. As Paz points out in his essay, "The translator's point of departure is not language in movement, the poet's raw material, but the fixed language of the poem. . . . His operation is the reverse of the poet's: he doesn't construct an immovable text with movable signs, but takes the elements of the text apart, places the signs in circulation again, and returns them to language." I'd argue, however, that in the case of the student who clings to the literal, as well as the student imprisoned by his own expression, just such dismantlement and reconstruction is what is most direly needed. Simply by coming to see their experience and expression as "material" for their art, rather than the fixed granite of "original" creation, the literalist and the obfuscator will quickly be freed of their own defenses. Paz concludes by saying, "The ideal of poetry translation, according to a definition of Valéry's that cannot be improved upon, is to produce similar effects with different means." So, too, with "what really happened." Ditto the inwardness that may mean a great deal to the writer but has yet to open up to the reader through "different means."

Nothing, however, beats the immersion into the difficulties and challenges of translation itself in order to reveal to students the power and complexity of language. Unfailingly they sign up for translation workshop thinking that all they need do is translate each word "correctly" in order to come up with a sound translation, a sort of paint-by-numbers operation that will conjure the ready-made poem or story. Most of them in fact begin in just this way, spending hours and hours slaving over a dictionary in order to come up with just the right meaning of each and every word. Soon, however, they realize that language proficiency is only the start, and that the real challenge lies in reading deeply enough into the original in order to see what's really going on within it, and then to have the English "chops" ready to render it. The first part of this operation requires that they stand in shoes wholly other than their own, that through their reading they come to occupy the mind and inspiration of the original in much the same way that "listening" to those opening sentences of Hemingway's story reveals the marrow of Nick's feeling and thought. In short, the student translator must "another" his or her imagination in order to fully comprehend the Neruda or Rilke or Akhmatova they are about to let speak through them. This, however, is not simply a two-step operation, one where they comprehend the original and then translate it. Rather, as they begin to translate, only then do they fully discover what is going on in the original by realizing what they can and cannot render from it. Put another way, "Du mußt dein Leben ändern" may be easily understood in German, but the layers of its complexity are revealed even more clearly when the student tries to translate all that it is saying.

For when it comes to translation we really are talking about recreating the missing head and limbs of the living god. While their shape may be clearly rendered or invoked by the original, the same is not so easily done in the translation. For students of writing, the same can be said for what may seem palpable to them in either their experience or their imagination, but which still needs to be enhanced, heightened, manipulated, altered, emphasized, evoked, etc., in the writing itself. As a student recently noted in writing about translation, "I used to think that two or three drafts were enough for any piece of writing. Now, because of translation, I see it can take 20 or 25. It's a process that just never ends but only grows more fascinating (and frustrating!) as you go." In other words, through translation the student had become a better, more demanding writer in her own language. What she had come to see was that, ultimately, it was not simply her own language, but instead a "different means" to render "similar effects" in draft after draft after draft.

Frost famously stated that "Poetry is what gets lost in translation." However, while there is always some element of the original that remains at risk of disappearing, there is also a great deal that is found in translation as well. Here, for instance, is a short poem by Ingborg Bachmann:

Schatten Rosen Schatten

Unter einem fremden Himmel
Schatten Rosen
Schatten
auf einer fremden Erde
zwischen Rosen und Schatten
in einem fremden Wasser
mein Schatten

Here are various definitions of its key words:

Schatten – shadow, shadows, shade
Rosen – roses
Himmel – sky, heaven, heavens, Heaven
fremden – foreign, strange, other, alien, different
Erde – earth, Earth
Wasser – water

Given this outline, as well as the knowledge that "unter" and "zwischen" mean "under" and "between," respectively, anyone can translate this poem. However, anyone who begins to do so quickly realizes that it is impossible to know for sure when Bachmann intends "Schatten" to be plural or singular. Add to this the multiple definitions of "fremden," as well as the difference between rendering "Himmel" as "sky" or "Heaven," and one quickly enters the vertiginous fun house known as translation. Indeed, there is much that can't help but be lost, for English will not allow for such multiple meanings and forms in any of the possible words chosen.

But neither does German, for any German reader experiencing the poem must also make these same choices. While a German reader would indeed appreciate the two case forms at work in "Schatten," the same reader must also ultimately make a choice between the singular and plural in order to make sense of the poem. In other words, the fact that

"Schatten" is both singular and plural only becomes *meaningful* when the reader decides on precisely which it is at which particular point in the poem. This, then, becomes the reader's *reading* of the poem within the poem in much the same way that Rilke's poem strives to conjure the hidden visage of its god. *That* poem, or *that* god only exists in the reading, and it is this reading that translation ultimately seeks to lay hold of and render.

"Schatten Rosen Schatten" happens to be the first poem I translated when I began work on Ingeborg Bachmann in the summer of 1982. Here is the version I arrived at then and have stood by over the years:

Shadows Roses Shadow

Under an alien sky
shadows roses
shadow
on an alien earth
between roses and shadows
in alien waters
my shadow

I offer this here not as the best solution, for no translator can ever claim finality. Rather, if I feel the translation works, it's because I feel that I've arrived at a consistent reading that invokes or even uncovers the paradox at work in the original. Hence, the shift from the plural to the singular in the title, as well as the gradual move from the confusing multiplicity of "shadows" within the body of the poem to the speaker's identification of her singular "shadow" at the end. My preference for "alien" lies in the urge to escape the tinge of nationalism that clings to "foreign" or the vagueness of "strange." Instead, "alien" seems to me to grant an otherworldly, more metaphysical feeling, while the choices of "sky" and "earth" keep us anchored in the elements. My one sway from the quotidian is the use of plural "waters" at the end, though it's the choice I am most pleased by, for it links well with the metaphysical flavor of "alien," alludes to the multiple "shadows" the speaker feels lost within, and also carries with it the more threatening geopolitics inherent to "alien waters." In such manner I have my cake and eat it too by evoking the bleak Cold War world Bachmann speaks to in 1956 as well as outlining an existential crisis that is timeless.

Frost's edict then is right, but only locally so. For really the true poetry of Bachmann's poem lies in the journey from the words on the page to the poem that we construct within our imagination. While a certain kind of poem is constructed in German, another kind can also exist in English, one that even mimics the act of construction that takes place in the German, but in a different way. Though some part of poetry may indeed be lost in the journey from the original, this is only a call for another poetry to be invented or gained in the translation. Not that it always happens, to be sure, but in the reaching for it lies the effort at creation, one akin to the student's own need to move from the fixed parameters of experience or an early draft in order to attain a language that takes on a life of its own. This same sense of transformation is also what energizes the writer in me when I'm translating. By immersing myself in what Paz calls "a world of relations made of contradictions and correspondences, unions and separations," I not only feel enriched as a writer but more nimble in my ability to shape meaning through words. Returning to my own writing, the hard work of inspiration and generation is still there. Yet once a live poem is set in motion, because of translation the playing field feels more open, myself free to move in any direction that will help me to better see where the writing itself is meant to go.

Translation is a humbling art, but not an art of defeat. Instead, wrestling with the shades and complexities of language, be it a foreign language or one's own, only heightens the humility that all writers come to feel in the face of expression itself. As the experienced writer is well aware, it is one thing to say something clearly or accurately, quite another to say it artfully and truthfully as well. The effort requires a willingness to continually make and remake what Stevens expressed so well as "The poem of the mind in the act of finding/ What will suffice." Through translation, or at the very least by considering what the process of translation might reveal to them, students come to see that "the act of finding" is inherent and perpetual to their craft, that their roles as creators are more consequential than what they may initially have believed, and that indeed their lives are "changed" forever once they realize the potential for being remade by their art.

ESSAY

Stephen Collington
The Anyone-Can-Do-It Method for Writing Chinese Poetry (in Japanese)
Thoughts on Language, Authenticity and Form

Okay, let's get right down to business and write a poem in Chinese.

It won't take long: just four lines, five characters per line, twenty characters in total. Our guide for the process will be Nitta Daisaku, late professor of literature at Jissen Women's University, Tokyo, Japan. We join him in mid-lecture, on page 92 of his popular 1970 handbook *How to Write Chinese Poetry* (Kanshi no tsukurikata):

> . . . so setting aside the finicky details, let's start, as always, with some word-searching in the Poetic Diction Dictionary. This time, why don't we change our perspective a bit with something like "sending off a friend" or "partings"?
>
> Choosing autumn for the season, I take a long look at "Autumn: Partings" (page 231). Various scenes, suggested by the words and phrases there, float about in the mind. The phrase "lingering moon" catches my attention. Sending a friend off, remaining behind alone afterwards—some such scene would seem to go with 殘月 "lingering moon." Why don't we try it?
>
> Vaguely thinking along those lines, I continue searching. I wonder what's available for rhymes, so I take a look there. Under "Rhyme 5: 微" the phrase 白雲飛 "white clouds above us soar" pops out at me. That would go well with the "lingering moon" from earlier, wouldn't it. Let's try it:
>
> > lingering moon   white clouds above us soar
>
> The meter is ○● ●○◎. That should fit nicely—let's go with that. Since it ends on a rhyme ◎, it will have to be an even-numbered line, second or last. Let's make it last for now: those soaring clouds seem to invite us to large and distant thoughts, so if we think of our third or "turn" line in those terms, they should come together quite well for a conclusion.
>
> Looking at the "Turn Line Endings" chart with that in mind, we see various possibilities:
>
>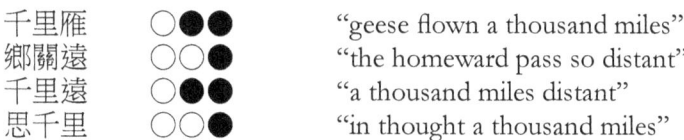
>
> | | | |
> |---|---|---|
> | 千里雁 | ○●● | "geese flown a thousand miles" |
> | 鄉關遠 | ○○● | "the homeward pass so distant" |
> | 千里遠 | ○●● | "a thousand miles distant" |
> | 思千里 | ○○● | "in thought a thousand miles" |
>
> etc.
>
> The meter here of course has to be ○●●, so we need to use "geese flown a thousand miles" or "a thousand miles distant" or the like. But what about the start of the line? Bringing out the explicit object of the "thoughts of return" might be a good way to go. . . .

And so, thinking this way and that, I settle at last on 故山千里遠 ●○ ○●● "old mountain home a thousand miles distant" for the turn at line three. Putting together the results so far:

故山千里遠
殘月白雲飛

old mountain home   a thousand miles distant
lingering moon   white clouds above us soar

That should do.

So now it's time for our first and second lines. The second or "extension" line has to rhyme of course, and we used "Rhyme 5: 微" in our closing line, so back to "Rhyme 5: 微" we must go. The phrase 獨倚扉 "leaning against the door" jumps out. Left behind after the friend's departure, leaning against the door for support—a nice, lonely, desolate feeling to the words. Let's use it. The meter is ●●◎, so the first part of the verse has to be ○○ or ●○, or we'll be breaking the rules. But look, there's the phrase 送君 ●○ "I watch you go"—that would probably fit.

送君獨倚扉   ●○ ●●◎
I watch you go   leaning against the door

A faint feeling of desolation pervades the line: the friend departed; the poet left, finally, alone. If we're going to capitalize on it, however, we're probably going to need to mention the circumstances of "I watch you go" at some point in the poem. And of course, all we've got left to work with is the first line. So let's see. . . .

In the "Turn Line Endings" chart, there's a 催歸思 "your thoughts now turning homeward." Meter: ○○●. In a quatrain like the one we're writing, the first line must always end on a ●, so that will fit. (That's why we look in the "Turn Line Endings" chart—it has the line-end segments that end in ●.) So then the first part of the line has to be ○● or ●●. And right at the beginning of the lists, there it is: 遊子 ○● "wandering guest." Metrically that looks good, so let's line it up:

遊子催歸思   ○● ○○●
wandering guest   your thoughts now turning homeward

It's a little lacking in poetry, but maybe that's a good thing. If the poetic feeling is too ramped up from the start, one can sometimes run out of breath later.

Anyway, putting it all together . . .

wandering guest　　your thoughts now turning homeward

I watch you go　　leaning against the door

old mountain home　　a thousand miles distant

lingering moon　　white clouds above us soar

It's not that great, perhaps, but it feels more or less finished. When the moon lingers in the sky at dawn, the clouds that float past no doubt may look light or dark, depending on the weather, but then there's the old expression, "White clouds and thoughts of home." So I'll just have to beg for indulgence there. Title? How about, 送友人歸鄉 "Sending a Friend Off Home"? And don't forget to put the date on it. . . .

Kanshi no tsukurikata, pp. 92-4

Well, there are mysteries here to be sure—not least, all that talk of ○'s and ●'s in connection with "meter." The circles refer, of course, to the special tonal prosody of classical Chinese poetry, in which "level" tones (○ where the voice is held at a constant pitch) are contrasted with "deflected" tones (● where the voice rises or falls sharply) in various patterns. It may seem complicated at first, but all you really need to know in practice is a few basic rules:

(1) the second and fourth circle in each line must be different (_○_●_ or _●_○_), and that 2-4 pattern in turn must vary *between* lines in a prescribed way;

(2) there should never be three circles of the same type at the end of a line (_ _ ○○○ or _ _ ●●●);

(3) the fifth circle of lines two and four must be a ◎, which is considered a ○ for the purposes of rule (2) above (i.e., _ _ ○○◎ is disallowed).

And that's about it, at least for this type of quatrain. As for what the circles *mean*—what the various level ○ and deflected ● tones *really* sound like; how the patterns fit together to make a pleasing tonal prosody; even how the rhymes actually *do* rhyme sometimes (when it looks like they shouldn't)—all that can be set aside, as Professor Nitta would say, as just so much "finicky detail."

The basic outline of what he has done, at any rate, is clear. Drawing upon a special "Poetic Diction Dictionary," he has written a traditional, four-line Chinese quatrain, using separate charts for the ends of rhyming lines ("Rhyme 5: 微") and non-rhyming lines ("Turn Line Endings"), and a metrically annotated listing of words and phrases under the heading "Autumn: Partings" for everything else.

The result is a poem that meets all the requirements of a classical Chinese quatrain: it rhymes, and has its tones in the right places, and it follows the expected rise-extend-turn-tie pattern of development from one line to the next. If we could somehow travel back in time and ask Li Bai or Du Fu or the other Tang Dynasty masters their opinion, they might not be exactly bowled over by it . . . but nor would they find it the least bit strange.

So Professor Nitta has written a Chinese poem. And as the title of his book *How to Write Chinese Poetry* makes clear, he intends it as a demonstration for others interested in learning to do the same.

But that's still not the strange part.

The strange part is that Nitta is writing for an audience that (honorable exceptions aside) does not, for all practical purposes, speak a word of Chinese.

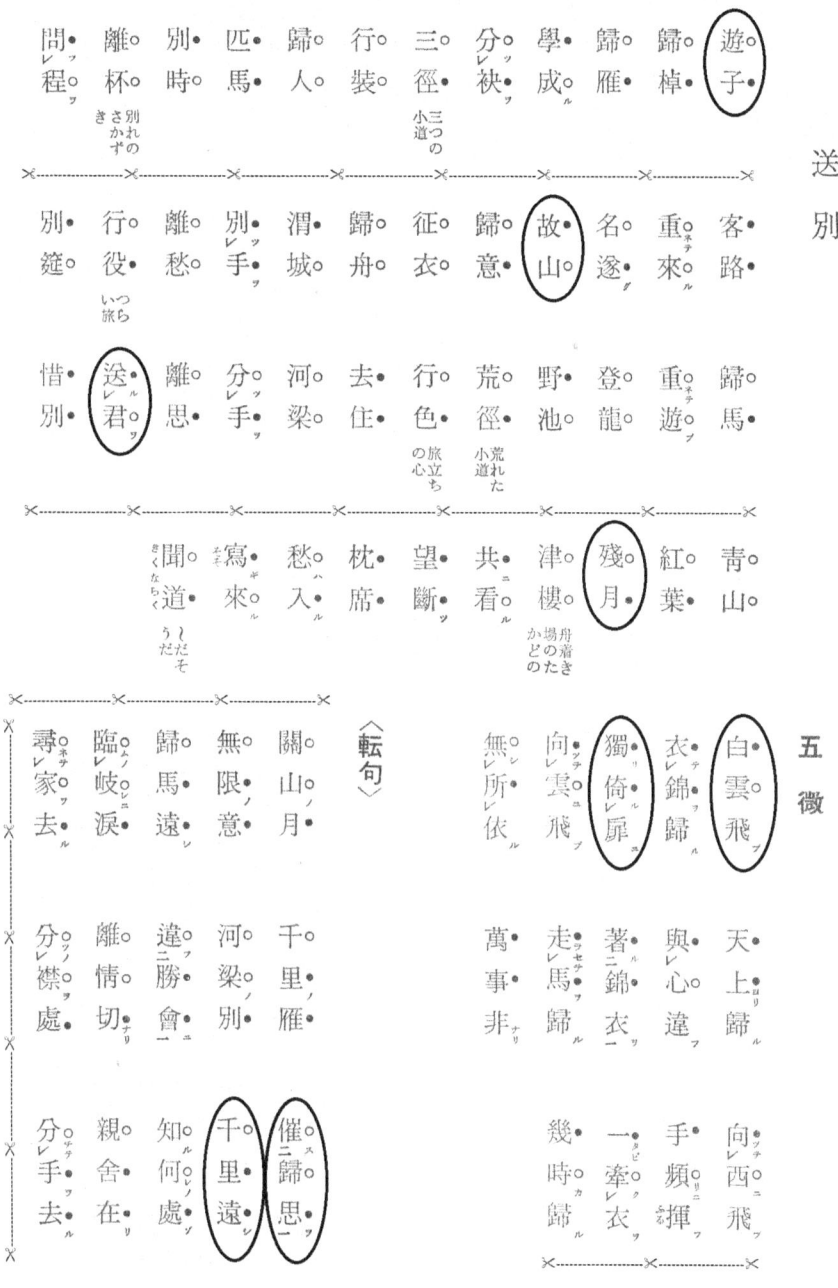

"Autumn: Partings" Main Vocabulary Chart, "Rhyme 5: 微" and "Turn Line Endings" (samples), from *Kanshi no tsukurikata*, pp. 231-8.

In his perennially popular 1959 textbook *How Does a Poem Mean?* John Ciardi first related an anecdote about W. H. Auden that has since gone on to become part of the shared folklore of the modern poetry workshop:

> W. H. Auden was once asked what advice he would give a young man who wished to become a poet. Auden replied that he would ask the young man why he wanted to write poetry. If the answer was "because I have something important to say," Auden would conclude that there was no hope for that young man as a poet. If on the other hand the answer was something like "because I like to hang around words and overhear them talking to one another," then that young man was at least interested in a fundamental part of the poetic process and there was hope for him. (*How Does a Poem Mean?* p. 3)

It makes for a nice image, the young poet quietly hanging around the parts of speech, taking notes on their conversations like some kind of lexical anthropologist. And most of us no doubt would be content to leave it at just that: a *nice image*—suggestive, slightly humorous, useful as a point of departure for thinking about how we write poetry, but hardly practical as a prescription for real training in the art. But what if we were to take the man at his word?

Nitta Daisaku does not mention Auden in *How to Write Chinese Poetry*, but he certainly would have agreed with him about the importance of hanging around with words and listening to them talk. And he has a very specific group of them in mind: the 240-page "Poetic Diction Dictionary" which makes up the bulk of his handbook. It is there, he insists, that the aspiring poet must start, discovering which words fit with which words, and what they say when they get together in groups:

> When writing Chinese poetry, it is essential to use a collection of poetic diction like the one included in this book, selecting appropriate words and phrases out of it, and practicing lining them up and fitting them together. . . . This practice in word gathering is the real foundation for writing Chinese poetry. . . . It may seem like terribly monotonous work, but in truth it is an unbeatable method for building strength. At the introductory stage, I earnestly entreat you to engage in this kind of training. (*Kanshi no tsukurikata*, pp. 82-84)

Of course, to Western readers, accustomed perhaps to more romantic ideas about poetic development ("poets are born, not made"), such a program might seem unduly restricting, even stultifying—especially after Nitta lets out how long he expects learners to spend at it before venturing beyond:

> Keep repeating this word gathering practice for several months, and when you've got the tone-meter patterns in your head, and more importantly, when you've come to feel in your heart that this word gathering stuff is actually kind of interesting, then you'll have graduated, more or less. (p. 84)

More than anything that we are told to do, however, it may be what we are told *not* to do that ultimately seems strangest from our Western perspective. For even if the restriction is implicit in the method itself, it's still a bit jarring to see it spelled out so baldly. Not only is the notion that the poet might have "something important to say" irrelevant to his process of word gathering, Nitta actively forbids it:

> You must never get the idea that you'll just try expressing your own private thoughts or poetic intention in Chinese characters. If that's what you're after, you should learn to write modern free verse, or some other form, but not Chinese poetry. (p. 84)

Auden, after all, never said that a poet should *not* have something important to say. The most that can be inferred from Ciardi's anecdote is that he believed that a lively interest in language—in *how* a given message might be conveyed, as opposed to the *what* of the message itself—is a better predictor of success. A poet's first interest, as a poet, should be poetry . . . but surely that doesn't preclude saying something personally significant along the way?

And it's not like this restriction on personal expression is simply a temporary expedient, something to keep the learner on task until the basics are mastered. No, for even after we have graduated ("more or less"!) from mere word gathering and turn the page to "Composition" to write our first poems, we still find Nitta sounding the same grim warning:

> I'll say it again: all inner demand for self-expression, all things related to so-called modern poetics, are absolutely forbidden at this time. (p. 85)

Can he be serious? The whole business really *is* starting to sound rather daft—the comically self-contradictory delusions of some tin-pot literary reactionary. The poet is brought forward, primed for the moment of poetic creation . . . and then told to suppress "all inner demand for self-expression." Logically speaking, it would seem that no poem at all could happen under such conditions. Where is the impetus for the thing supposed to come from? If not the poet, who is going to write the poem?

Why, the words will, of course. Go hang out with the words, is Professor Nitta's reply. *Listen to what* **they** *have to say.*

Of course, trying one's hand at poetry in a foreign language—and in a "dead" or classical variety of one at that—is a phenomenon by no means limited to the *kanshi* poets of Japan. Indeed, writing verses in Latin was for centuries an educational rite of passage for students in England, and later America and beyond.

And nor was it always a mere classroom exercise, something to be handed in and (hopefully) quickly forgotten. A complete edition of Milton's poems, for example, will contain a tidy sixty or seventy pages of Latin, not to mention sonnets in Italian and a translation of Psalm 114 into rolling Greek hexameters, à la Homer. There's even a letter to dad ("Ad Patrem"), presumably written after Milton senior had expressed disapproval of his son's post-graduation career path: "Nec tu vatis opus divinum despice carmen" (You should not despise the poet's task, divine song . . .) and so on for 120 lines. At least the old man would know he'd got his money's worth paying for all that fancy education!

So, no, we should not be too quick to judge: there's absurdity enough among peoples—and certainly among poets—to go around. There's even a Latin equivalent to Nitta's "Poetic Diction Dictionary," the *Gradus ad Parnassum*, a kind of poetical thesaurus for aspiring latter-day Virgils and Ovids. The two types of book differ in arrangement in important ways, but their underlying purpose is the same. Each provides a suitable selection of vocabulary for poetic composition, and crucially each shows the correct *metrical* value for every word presented, so that poets using them can be sure that their lines will scan correctly.

But then, if you don't even know how to pronounce the words you're using, what on earth is the point of writing verse—*metrical* verse—in a foreign language? It's as if poets in some far off land were to decide one day to write in English pentameters, but have no idea whatsoever where the accents fall. (Is it whatSOeVER or WHATsoeVER? Or *what*?)

Of course, one might suppose that all that looking up of words in Poetic Diction Dictionaries would at least leave poets with a clear sense of what the *final* result—their own work, after all—should sound like. But even there, common sense comes away baffled. As Derek Attridge has documented in *Well-Weighed Syllables*, his fascinating study of Elizabethan experiments with "quantitative" verse, the distinction between long and short syllables that is the foundation of classical Latin prosody was entirely lost on our literary ancestors. It didn't exist in English, or in any of the descendants of Latin that they knew (it had disappeared, in fact, long before Latin branched out into the modern Romance languages); and so with no model to work from, and no one to tell them differently, they simply assumed that the effect was inaudible:

> It was an intellectual apprehension, not an aural one. . . . He [the student/poet] probably accepted in good faith that others with acuter senses or finer minds than his had worked out which syllables were long and which short, and what kinds of pattern were the most challenging and the most satisfying . . . [b]ut his prosodical training led him far away from any conception of metre as a rhythmic succession of sounds . . . into a world pervaded by a sense of subtle intelligence and high civilization, where words are anatomized and charted with a precision and a certainty unknown in the crude vernacular. (*Well-Weighed Syllables*, pp. 76-7)

In the case of Japanese, of course, things are made even more complicated by the logographic writing system which it inherits from Chinese. To simplify somewhat in the interest of brevity, each written character in Chinese represents a single "word" (strictly speaking, *morpheme*) as an integral unit of *meaning + sound*. Naturally, however, only one of those elements, *meaning*, is readily translatable between languages. The Japanese people's historical solution to that dilemma—a choice whose awkward, maddening, yet also beautiful consequences they live with to this day—was just to reassign the characters to native (Japanese) words, according to their meanings.

Character	Basic Meaning	Loan-word Chinese Pronunciation	Reassigned Japanese Pronunciation
送	send	sō	oku(ru)
君	you	kun	kimi
獨	alone	doku	hito(ri)
倚	lean	i	yo(ru)
扉	door	hi	tobira

One happy result of this compromise is that Japanese readers can often look at a passage of Chinese and make a fairly good guess as to its meaning, familiar as they are with the basic store of characters from everyday use. But then, Chinese and Japanese work on radically different grammatical principles—particularly in the matter of word order—so it still looks like a bit of a jumble. Reading the characters with their reassigned Japanese pronunciation is halfway along to a translation anyway; why stop there? Why not just rearrange the word order so that the line makes better sense in Japanese?

And that, of course, is exactly what they do. Using a small number of rule-of-thumb principles, an experienced reader can take a line of Chinese poetry, and swiftly turn it inside out and upside down, so that it reads in a rough-and-ready, but generally serviceable variety of Japanese. Verbs are shifted so that they fall *after* the direct object, and various inflections and grammatical particles, absent in the original, are quietly added. And so it is that the second line of Professor Nitta's poem, what we have seen translated above as

    I watch you go   leaning against the door

goes from being

    ¹送   ²君   ³獨   ⁴倚   ⁵扉

    <u>sō</u>   <u>kun</u>   <u>doku</u>   <u>i</u>   <u>hi</u>

to

    ²君を   ¹送りて   ³獨り   ⁵扉に   ⁴倚る

    <u>kimi</u> o   <u>okurite</u>   <u>hitori</u>   <u>tobira</u> ni   <u>yo</u>ru

in the blink of a reader's eye.

Even if the Japanese pronunciation of direct *loan words* preserved some trace of the tone accents of the original Chinese—which it doesn't, no more than the English pronunciation of loan words preserves the long and short vowels of classical Latin—it wouldn't matter. Once the line actually comes to be read out loud, the carefully reproduced tonal meter of Tang Dynasty poetry goes right out the window. The whole line has been reshuffled, rearranged, *repronounced*. Even the rhyme which Professor Nitta was so careful to place at the end of the verse is gone.

    Really, it can't be emphasized too strongly: this is not some occasional or optional trick; this is how Japanese readers habitually *read* Chinese poems, including the ones which they themselves have written. In other words, Professor Nitta's book explains how to write metrically correct, rhymed *Chinese* poetry to Japanese readers who, should they take him up on the challenge, will never so much as hear the meter or the rhyme of their own poems . . . and that for the simple reason that they'll never actually read them in Chinese.

One wonders what, say, John Keats would have made of it all. It's hard to imagine that this was quite the sort of thing he had in mind when he wrote his famous ode, but there you are. The Japanese *kanshi* poet takes the tonal music of classical Chinese poetry and turns it into something altogether liberated from the demands of the mere "sensual" ear:

> Heard melodies are sweet, but those unheard
> Are sweeter; therefore, ye soft pipes, play on;
> Not to the sensual ear, but more endear'd,
> Pipe to the spirit ditties of no tone. . . .
>
> ("Ode on a Grecian Urn")

It's a lovely idea, really. But then, as we have seen, in practice it involves months of lonely training with the Poetic Diction Dictionary and a rigorous suppression of "all inner demand for self-expression" . . . and even then the results may well be, as Professor Nitta puts it, "not that great, perhaps."

And so the question remains, Why bother? Why go to all that trouble matching tone and rhyme patterns in blind obedience to an alien prosody, when you'll never actually *hear* the tones and the rhymes when you read your finished poem? Why, in short, even attempt to write Chinese poetry at all?

One answer to that last question, of course, would just be *because you can*. As we have seen above, in its relationship with Chinese, Japanese is a lot like English, in its relationship with Latin. But while we may be able to look at a line of Latin verse and pick out much that seems oddly familiar ("Nec *tu* ['Et **tu**, Brute!'] *vatis* [vatic] *opus* [opus] *divinum* [divine] *despice* [despise/**despic**able] *carmen* [Miranda?] . . ."), no one imagines that you can actually read the stuff with understanding—let alone write it—without extensive training in Latin as a foreign language. The grammar is just too complicated. Even when all the words *are* familiar (and Milton's line is probably exceptional in that regard), it will generally be impossible to see the relationships between them.

With Chinese, however, things are very different. While it's a mistake to assert—as has indeed sometimes been done—that Chinese is a language "without grammar," it's not hard to see how the misunderstanding itself could arise:

遊	子	催	歸	思
travel	person	urge	return	thought
送	君	獨	倚	扉
send	you	alone	lean	door
故	山	千	里	遠
old	mountain	thousand	mile	distant
殘	月	白	雲	飛
remnant	moon	white	cloud	fly

Starting with a language already marked by "analytic" spareness—a language without inflections or tenses or cases or gender or number—the poets of classical China took the logic of juxtaposition to its ultimate natural conclusion. Ruthlessly stripping away all "superfluous" connecting material, they produced, in effect, a kind of self-contained literary dialect based on radical simplicity and suggestion. It is not "without grammar"—syntactic relationships are still governed, fundamentally, by Chinese word order—but compared to the complexities of an inflected, "synthetic" language like Latin, it almost might as well be.

And so it is that Japanese readers can look at a poem in the Tang Dynasty style and not only understand it (if, sometimes, in a rough-and-ready way), but even aspire to emulate it. The simplicity of the poetry itself is part of the attraction. With "grammar" reduced, practically speaking, to a principle of juxtaposition, the text becomes a series of leaps—from image to image and thought to thought—that can seem at times to take in entire worlds ... and all in the space of as few as twenty Chinese characters.

It looks so easy ... as if anyone could do it. And indeed—it's not a joke—there really *is* an "anyone-can-do-it" method, Tachikake Rozan's *The Anyone-Can-Do-It Method for Writing Chinese Poetry (With Complete Poetic Diction)*, sharing pride of place on the shelf beside Professor Nitta's *How to Write Chinese Poetry*. ("Can anyone write Chinese poetry?" Tachikake asks on the first page of his book. "The answer is simple: Anyone can.")

And yet, again, the obvious objection remains. If everything is so very easy, why should anyone need a handbook in the first place?

It's an interesting puzzle in literary psychology. A Japanese poet who wanted to try capturing something of the imagistic verbal magic of the Tang Dynasty masters really could just go ahead and write. The words, thanks to more than a thousand years of borrowing from China, are familiar enough after all. Why not, as Professor Nitta puts it, "just try expressing your own private thoughts or poetic intention in Chinese characters"? Juxtapose this image with that, make an unexpected turn at line 3, open out to wider prospects for a suitably expansive close—with a little practice, surely, one could soon be doing Li Bai proud.

Mindless formalism? What else can one call it, this insistence that one *must* follow the rules, that one's lines *must* scan with the correct tonal prosody, and rhyme in the right class of rhymes? If neither poet nor potential audience will ever hear those effects in the finished poem, what is the point of the exercise?

Authenticity? Well, yes. To write a rhymed, prosodically correct poem in Tang Dynasty Chinese—that's one kind of "authenticity." And if you're going to write "Chinese poetry," perhaps it really is the one kind that counts. Otherwise, as Professor Nitta puts it, what you wind up with might be "modern free verse, or some other form," but it won't be "*Chinese* poetry" in anything like the desired sense of the term.

But then, if we drop the word "Chinese" for a moment and think only in terms of what we normally mean by "poetry," the procedure really does seem rather mad. The poet sits and sorts through a list of preselected vocabulary, arranged, for convenience, by topic and metrical value and rhyme, and cobbles a poem together according to what pattern fits where in the established form. Where's the room for the authentic voice of experience in that?

Again, however, comes the answer, from Professor Nitta, from the many devoted *kanshi* poets of modern Japan: *The authentic voice of experience* **is** *the words.*

> The resulting work . . . might seem to some to be removed from reality—ever so behind the times—but in truth it is not so. . . . Literature, ultimately, is a kind of *lie*, a fiction. And yet, even while being fiction, it does not stop at being fiction, but is at the same time an expression of the truth of its author. Let us suppose that we have some *thing* portrayed here: the thing portrayed, then, is none other than a projection of the person who made the portrait, nothing less than an expression of that person's inner self. Moreover, there's something mysterious and wonderful about the fact that in doing so one brings into being a world that one had otherwise never so much as imagined before. This, it seems to me, is a pleasure that can be said to belong to the writing of Chinese poetry alone.
>
> *Kanshi no tsukurikata*, p. 90

It is the paradox of form—and in the starkest terms. You choose some *formal* element of language to foreground in a poem, and in doing so, you drastically restrict the linguistic options available to you. Inevitably, often repeatedly, you find yourself diverted from what you "really" had to say when you started, denied the use of one verb because it doesn't rhyme, pushed towards some other because it does, and so on. At some level, you really do have to suppress your "inner demand for self-expression" and just listen instead to the words.

The process has its perils and its pitfalls, to be sure. In the clamor of voices that is the "Poetic Diction Dictionary," it can take a sensitive ear to pick out the truly interesting conversations between words—and a strong will, too, to resist the more obvious and banal suggestions they sometimes make. And ultimately, of course, the only meaningful standard of success is whether the final result is a poem worth reading—a test that's not easy to pass in any language.

At any rate, Professor Nitta's defense of literature as fiction is perhaps the final clue we need to understand the Anyone-Can-Do-It Method, and its perennial appeal. If you are "Sending a Friend Off Home," is it more authentic to describe the noise and the crush of Tokyo Station, the smell of the lunchboxes on sale at the kiosks, the low whine—then roar—of the Bullet Train as it pulls away from the platform . . . or to set yourself leaning against the door of an old thatched cottage, watching the "wandering guest" slowly disappear into the distance, as the crescent moon fades and white clouds soar, high above in the morning sky?

The answer, of course, is that it will depend—on the poet, and on the poem that results, and on the sympathies of that poem's potential readers. But certainly there seems no reason to deny either approach out of hand. And besides, it's hard to disagree with Professor Nitta when he says that there is something "mysterious and wonderful" about a poetry that allows—indeed, *forces*—its practitioners to leave their day-to-day world behind, and explore instead scenes and places "never so much as imagined before."

The night is calm, the moon glitters upon the river . . . and there beneath a tree, Li Bai beckons with a jug of wine. Go on. *Anyone can do it*.

Just don't forget your flashlight. You're going to need it to use the Poetic Diction Dictionary.

Sources

Aler, Paul, et al. *Gradus ad Parnassum; sive novum synonymorum, epithetorum, versuum, ac phrasium poeticarum thesaurus.* London: Company of Stationers, 1817. (First published 1686. Accessed via Google Books, March 2010.)

Attridge, Derek. *Well-Weighed Syllables: Elizabethan Verse in Classical Metres.* Cambridge University Press, 1974.

Ciardi, John and Miller Williams. *How Does a Poem Mean?* Second edition. Boston: Houghton Mifflin, 1975 (1959).

Nitta Daisaku, *Kanshi no tsukurikata: Kindai Nihon Kanshi-ron e no josetsu.* Meiji shoin, 1970. （新田大作『漢詩の作り方 －近代日本漢詩論への序説－』明治書院、1970。） Translated title: *How to Write Chinese Poetry: Preface to a Theory of Chinese Poetry in Modern Japan.*

(Rozan) Tachikake Shigeo, *(Shigo kambi) Dare ni mo dekiru Kanshi no tsukurikata*, Rozan shisho kankōkai, 1990 (1963). （呂山　太刀掛重男『詩語完備・だれにもできる漢詩の作り方』呂山詩書刊行会、1990、初版 1963。） Translated title: *The Anyone-Can-Do-It Method for Writing Chinese Poetry (With Complete Poetic Diction).*

Shawcross, John T., ed. *The Complete Poetry of John Milton.* New York: Anchor Books, 1971.

Gilbert Wesley Purdy

The Quonset Hut

It was my grandparent's Quonset hut, but changed,
the floor no longer sand but soil, and where
the boxes filled with calico, arranged
along the walls, toys, bedspreads, ironware,
went on some thirty yards, that, to a child,
seemed almost endless, other wonders now
astonished me, lush tropical bowers wild
with flowers, gaping holes, shreds dangling down.

Where ribs were reft of corrugated sheets
a light poured past the jagged steel to daze
each thing within to silence, to replete—
where past and shadow used to loiter days—
each surface and the moment with itself.
A table held some books I'd meant to read,
surfaces laved with perfect light, as well.
I lingered knowing I must choose to leave.

Jamie Iredell

The Slot Tech

My father ran all the casino slots,
Checking every hopper, making the change
For gamblers, like fields flooded in spring rains,
Silver in the pastures of their winnings' cup.

Checking every hopper, making the change,
His radio blaring a sports book loss,
Silver in the endless casino's cup,
Gamblers' teamers torn to the floor in loss.

His radio blaring a sports book loss,
You'd never know his wager on roulette.
Gamblers' teamers torn to the floor in loss,
But my father knew how to place a bet.

You'd never know his wager on roulette.
If black always won his bet was on red,
But my father knew how to place a bet.
Because black would lose and then there's red.

If black always won his bet was on red,
While checking every hopper, making change.
Then black would lose and he won on red,
As long as the ball never settled on green.

While checking every hopper, making change
For gamblers, like fields flooded in spring rains,
Silver in the pastures of their winnings' cup,
My father ran all the casino slots.

Maryann Corbett

A Cautionary Tale

All wrong from the beginning. A mistake
I should have had the mother-wit to see:
she seventeen, and he
in the full seventeenth-century sense, a rake

progressing. Well along, in sober fact.
But at his best so *saveable*. Or so
I dreamed he might be; little did I know.
In feeble bleats of tact,

I let their doomed coach drive until it crashed
on the rainy, cobbled road of mismatched hearts—
his Gin Lane and her Beer Street, equal parts.
Cut to the present: he's sliced from her future, slashed,

out of her past. Now, like a troubled dream,
who's drifted through? Who's left a plastic sack
here on the stoop in back
with the favorite childhood toy she'd given him?

Stuffed tiger, slightly dirty, matted nap.
Pinned to it, there's a note
in the florid hand I recognize. My throat
clamps on the hopeless drama of this scrap-

scrawled misery. *How hard it is to bear,*
this toy. It keeps him dwelling on her, thinking.
Giving it back will help him swear off drinking.
He'll keep his distance. She won't run into him here.

Yes, he, ghost of my dangerous error past:
reckless romantic, brooding drunk, half-assed
loser of jobs, come back to his old haunts.
What no smart woman wants:

a lurch in the trajectory of her climb
on the far-off academic funhouse ride.
I bring the bag inside.
I never phone to say I've heard from him,

but drop the toy at Goodwill—and devise
strange circuits to avoid a certain street,
nervous that I might meet
those Byron ringlets and those madman eyes

in a wild face that would trail me to my door.
I might. There are no Bedlams anymore.

ESSAY

Marilyn L. Taylor
Semi-Formal Verse and Its Prosody

Over the course of the past several decades, it appears that a subtle, unacknowledged stylistic shift has been taking place in poetry before our very eyes—a phenomenon that has managed to substantially blur the boundaries that separate free verse from formal. Many of the poems that confront us now in the literary journals seem unclassifiable as one or the other, but fall instead into a new, quasi-metrical category that welcomes the better elements of both. Such poems have been referred to, in fact, as "semi-formal verse"—i.e. poetry that does not adhere strictly to the rules and restrictions of conventional prosody, but that never strays too far from them, either. Due to the increasing presence of such poetry, it would seem an appropriate time to take a look at it, investigate what it is, and make an attempt to predict its probable future.

I'll begin on the more slippery side of the slope, if I may, with the prosody of free verse—which, until relatively recently, scarcely anyone considered in terms of its prosodic elements. Matters such as lineation, rhythmic regularity, stress-count per line, and other such minutiae hadn't been seen as particularly relevant, except, perhaps, to committed linguists. For most of us, the automatic assumption has been that only poetry that is clearly *metrical* should suffer close rhythmic analysis at all. Why? Because unmetered poetry seems basically impossible to scan.

Back in 1935, for instance, in his book titled *Language as Gesture: Essays in Poetry*, R. P. Blackmur maintained that with many free-verse poets (D. H. Lawrence served as his object-lesson in this particular essay), "the very intensity of self-expression overwhelm[s] all other considerations, and the disorder alone prevail[s]." Elsewhere: "Lawrence submitted the obsessions of his experience to the heightening fire of hysteria, and put down the annealed product just as it came." And furthermore: "Hardy would have been ashamed of the lopsided, uneven metrical architecture."

It's clear where Blackmur's aesthetic proclivities lay at that time, although he must have known by then that he was fighting a losing battle—even while targeting a number of free-verse poets, Lawrence among them, to serve as the whipping-boys and girls for his particular (dying) point of view.

In the end, of course, it was that very "annealed product"—free verse—that became, overwhelmingly, the norm for American and English poetry. The trend gained considerable momentum in the decades following the Second World War, until the poets who would have been commended by Blackmur as "the metrical descendents of Hardy"—the likes of Frost, Millay, Teasdale, Brooks, Merrill, Wilbur, others— were simply dismissed, ignored, and even scorned by the literary tastemakers of the day.

Not surprisingly, this distinct and rather sudden swing of the pendulum from "metrical architecture" to "disorder" was noticed and written about by many critics and literary scholars. It was either the best thing in the world (*freedom!*) or the worst thing that could possibly have happened to poetry (*chaos!*), and the clamor on both sides resounded well into the nineteen-seventies and beyond.

For a time, all of this antagonism was seen as exciting, even if occasionally infuriating. What's more fun, academically speaking, than a small revolution within the ranks? A few skirmishes between the shaggy free-verse stalwarts vs. the tweedy New Formalists? Their disagreements, solemnly written up in journals that included, among others, *APR, Hudson Review,* and *Fence,* became known as the Poetry Wars (which in some quarters are still being fought, but mostly by undergraduates encountering the Beats for the very first time). It was gradually becoming clear, however, that where one came down on these issues was not merely a matter of one's presumed "philosophy" or even one's "politics" (in a ludicrous extension of the argument), but one of competing prosodic approaches, as well. A genuine need was developing for an impartial, intelligent analysis of what, exactly, had changed so drastically in English-language poetry over the course of less than half a century, and was continuing to change .

That need was finally addressed in 1980 with the publication of an extraordinary study by Charles O. Hartman titled *Free Verse: An Essay On Prosody.* It is a splendid take on the "mechanics" of free verse, and a convincing argument in support of the conviction that it is syntax and lineation that govern the rhythmic experience of a poem in the absence of regular meter.

Hartman, who pays considerable attention in his book to Williams, Larkin, and especially to Eliot, successfully lays to rest the Blackmurian idea that the rhythms of free verse are somehow "primitive," random, or impossible to analyze.

Conversely, the book also takes issue with those who believe that rhythmic regularity automatically leads to excessive artifice and rhythmic monotony. Thus no one from either camp goes home without the need for some degree of accountability.

What seems undeniable is this: in the thirty years since the publication of Hartman's text, an undeniable lull, if not a truce, in the poetry wars has taken place, along with an increasing willingness for the two sides to coexist peacefully. I can't say that the book was directly responsible for this trend, but I do suggest that it was a harbinger of more tolerant times to come. It actually does appear as though a new laissez-faire attitude is affecting American and English poetry scholarship at the present time, along with a discernable blending—or at least a more comfortable commingling—of styles, formerly wildly disparate, in the poems we're confronting in the latest journals and anthologies. Simultaneously, a distinct new prosodic hybrid seems to be emerging in the middle of it all.

This new sub-subgenre probably owes its genesis to the more liberal proponents of the New Criticism, and to practitioners of what Graham Hough back in 1960 called "Vers Libéré", which is not to be confused with "Vers Libre". *Vers Libéré*, according to Hough, is poetry that is technically free verse, but remains very much informed by traditional meters—unlike "vers libre", which for the most part is not.

I will interrupt myself at this point to emphasize that there is nothing new about shifting developments and fashions in poetry. Today's changes are merely a sign, I think, of how the prosodic pendulum—which has never stood still—may have reached the far side of "liberation", so to speak, from meter. And ever so slightly, it's beginning to swing back in the opposite direction. (One sure sign: the recent proliferation in the critical literature of descriptors like "anecdotal" and "disjunctive", used pejoratively.)

Many readers will recall that almost exactly the same thing happened precisely a century ago. Back in 1912, when Ezra Pound successfully nudged the pendulum in the direction of free verse, he did so by insisting upon something he called "absolute rhythm" in poetry. He urged poets to do away entirely with formal metrical conventions, all of which he considered impediments to the sincere expression of emotion. However, there were a significant number of American and British poets who, consciously or unconsciously, didn't buy the whole package. Think of Masters, Lindsay, Millay, Cummings, Teasdale and Wylie, for example. Despite what many of their more avant-garde contemporaries were doing, the work of these poets was still clearly informed by the conventions of meter. Taking into consideration such elements as the regular placement of stress, the use of rhyme, the uniformity of the line-length, and patterns of repetition, it's apparent that even Lawrence owed a great deal—although clearly not everything—to traditional versification.

Not surprisingly, Lawrence never overtly acknowledged using formal devices in his work. He might have had his critics in mind, but it's also possible that his use of the conventions was unconscious. In a revealing letter to his friend the anthologist Edward

Marsh, he said of his own rhythmic approach: "I think I read my poetry more by length than by stress—as a matter of movements in space, rather than footsteps hitting the earth." But in reality, any careful reader of Lawrence will hear the footsteps anyway. His lines may seldom manifest a regular backbeat, like the pentameters of Frost or Millay, but they can hardly be referred to as haphazard "movements in space" either. One critic, the metrist Hebe Riddick Bair, puts it this way:

"[Lawrence] uses traditional feet as a base meter, extended feet as a variation played against that base, and combinations of these as a third variation played against both." A demonstration: the first four lines of "The Ship of Death"—that lovely and rather grim extended meditation on mortality that Lawrence wrote in 1929, soon after he learned that he himself was dying:

> Now it is autumn and the falling fruit
> and the long journey towards oblivion.
> The apples falling like great drops of dew
> to bruise themselves an exit from themselves.

The excerpt clearly establishes the iambic pentameter as its "base meter". It features variations, but not radical ones, not the sort that would preclude the use of traditional foot-scansion; but they seem to suggest there will be further irregularities to come. And they do. In fact, the effect of reading the entire poem is not unlike examining one of those unsettling illustrations that demonstrate optical illusions. For a moment you think you're looking at the outline of a symmetrical vase or urn, and then you blink, and the whole thing has turned into a woman's head in profile.

This rather pleasant sense of disorientation was apparent in the work of a number of poets who were publishing between the late nineteen-twenties and the onset of World War II. Think, first, of Eliot's gradual defection from the free-verse movement, beginning with "The Waste Land" and culminating, metrically speaking, with "Four Quartets." Others of that era who rejected the sovereignty of free verse included Cummings, Bogan, Millay, MacLeish, and the Fugitive Poets of the American South. The work coming from these poets at that time wasn't exactly "free", but much of it wasn't exactly formal, either; it was both. Here was a hybrid prosody, which brought to vers libre a singular musicality and grace that had been missing for some time.

The interlude of coexistence ended quickly, however. In her insightful 1993 volume titled *The Ghost of Meter*, poet and critic Annie Finch acknowledges that "[t]hrough the 1930s . . . poets built on Eliot's idea of meter as a constant presence lurking behind the arras of free verse" (129), but she adds that in the decades that immediately followed World War II, free verse "lost touch with its metrical history" (130).

Using Sexton as her example, Finch further notes that meter was "accessible enough . . .

to reject with relative ease" (131). In other words, Sexton and many of her contemporaries were deeply familiar with the traditions and with the rules of traditional prosody, but chose to disregard them. Free verse had indeed won out, and was commencing its decades-long domination of the prosodic landscape. The era of coexistence had clearly ended.

Fashions in poetry, however—as in all of the arts—are cyclical, and an eventual move into the next phase was inevitable. Therefore, after thirty years of near-invisibility, poems in traditional forms—contemporary sonnets, villanelles, rondeaux, etc.—began to emerge again in the late nineteen-seventies and especially in the early eighties, much as they had back in the twenties. So frequently were they appearing in print, in fact, that in 1986 Philip Dacey & David Jauss published their splendid anthology featuring the best of them, entitled *Strong Measures*.

The more prolific and skilled of these poets—e.g. Timothy Steele, Charles Martin, Dana Gioia, Brad Leithauser, Mary Jo Salter and Mark Jarman, among a number of others—soon became identified as the New Formalists, and were either praised extravagantly or severely taken to task for their traditional aesthetic, which was referred to as both "groundbreaking" and "retrograde", depending upon the predilections of the critic. In the end, however, formalism thrived, and finally became recognized as a respectable alternative approach to writing poems. The early nineteen-nineties indeed saw what amounted to the completion of a fifty-year cycle, which began during the heyday of free verse, and ended with the acceptance, albeit occasionally grudging, of contemporary poetry in meter.

Now, however, as we enter the second decade of the 21st century, a new cycle appears to be gaining some momentum, very different in character from what came before. The earlier cycle, of course, began at a time when formal elements were finding their way into free verse; today's appears to be evolving the other way around.

In the current variation, the still-precarious foothold of rule-bound "formal" poetry is being artfully undermined by a looser, less obedient aesthetic. Just a few of its practitioners include Molly Peacock, Andrew Hudgins, Kim Addonizio, and Marie Ponsot—whose 1988 sonnet, titled "Out of Eden", was ahead of its time. It is provided here as an example of formal verse that is being consciously subverted by the poet herself:

Under the May rain over the dug grave	a
my mother is given canticles and I who believe	b
in everything watch flowers stiffen to new bloom.	c
Behind us the rented car fabricates a cave.	a
My mother nods: Is he? He is. But, is? Nods.	d
Angels shoo witches from this American tomb.	c

> The nod teaches me. It is something I can save.   a
> He left days ago. We, so that we too may leave,   b
> install his old belongings in a bizarre new room.   c
> I want to kneel indignantly anywhere and rave.   a
>
> Well, God help us, now my father's will is God's.   d
> At games and naming he beat Adam. He loved his Eve.   b
> I knew him and his wicked tongue. What he had, he gave.   a
>
> I do not know where to go to do it, but I grieve.   b

A scansion of the first three lines yields the following:

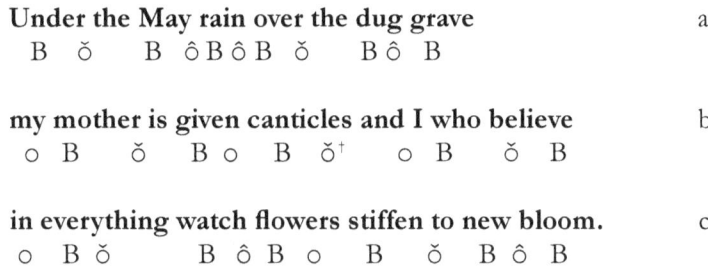

Please note, incidentally, that the scansion method being used here is based upon the system of beats and offbeats devised by the brilliant metrist Derek Attridge. Analyzing these lines via classical foot scansion can certainly be done, but the result might be counter-intuitive at best, near-gibberish at worst. A traditional analysis of the first line alone, perhaps, might serve to illustrate this claim quite clearly:

> *Under the May rain over the dug grave*

—a ten-syllable line. That implicative number, coupled with the overall "look" of the poem on the page, might subtly suggest that this is the beginning of a sonnet, and that we are about to confront the traditional iambic pentameter. However, the only genuine iamb in the line occurs in the position of the second foot. The other four feet all require substitutions, reversals, fusions, truncations, or coalitions.

---

†   Represents a three-syllable offbeat.

It can also be argued (if foot-scansion is used for the analysis) that the line consists entirely of two "extended" double-iambs. This may be correct. Or perhaps "under the" and "over the" are both dactyls, and "May rain" and "dug grave" are both spondees, so there are therefore only four feet in the line altogether. This could be correct, too. These several acceptable metrical analyses of the line show exactly why traditional scansion does not succeed here, and the Attridge system does.

To return to the poem itself: it's interesting to note how Ponsot toys here with the structure of the sonnet. Ostensibly Petrarchan, it really isn't, quite. The poem is divided into five sections—most unusual for a sonnet; and the rhyme scheme is aberrational, but not at all arbitrary: abc, adc, abca, dba, b.

But for all that, "Out of Eden" is a far cry from free verse. For one thing, it consists of fourteen lines. For another, it presents a recognizable, if not quite conventional, rhyme scheme. The clincher: it features a discernable sonnet-like "turn" between the tenth and eleventh lines. Nor is the poem an example of what Dana Gioia has called "pseudo-formal" poetry, i.e. free verse that has been tricked out with regularly recurring stanza breaks and uniform line-lengths for the sole purpose of achieving an attractively symmetrical, "formal" look on the page. (See Gioia's astute 1991 essay titled *Notes on the New Formalism* for more on this issue.) The care that Ponsot took to retain certain aspects of the sonnet form while eliminating others would seem to eliminate this possibility.

Rather, the poem appears to be an amalgam, a fusion, a "semi-formal" poem. It owes a great deal to traditional prosody, but it also exploits the expressive potential of free verse, achieving for itself a middle-of-the-road flexibility that retains much of the grace of form, along with the unstudied aesthetic of vers libre.

Is "Out of Eden" more successful by virtue of its reluctance to conform, by refusing to wear the traditional tuxedo to the poetry prom? Probably. It is, after all, a poem that expresses indignity, anger, despair. The speaker seems in no mood to follow old conventions to the letter, even though she is loosely bound by them: "Well, God help us," she grumbles—"now my father's will is God's."

There are countless other contemporary poems of this kind in print. I've listed a very few of them below, and more are being published every year. I do not intend to imply that their looser prosodic character will succeed in outshining the poetry that adheres to all of the rules of form. Nor will these poems have much of a chance of toppling the dominance of free verse. But I do suggest that such poems are already re-defining and enlarging the scope and breadth of what we think of nowadays as "formal poetry".

I further suggest that they may well encourage the use of a newer and vastly more practical mechanism than foot-scansion for the prosodic study of contemporary verse—the Attridge system—which allows those of us who are interested in such things to more easily keep tabs on the latest developments. Finally, I predict that this carefully "integrated" manner of writing will help usher in a new willingness to accommodate poetry's infinite variety—present, past, and still unwritten.

★ ★ ★

APPENDIX I

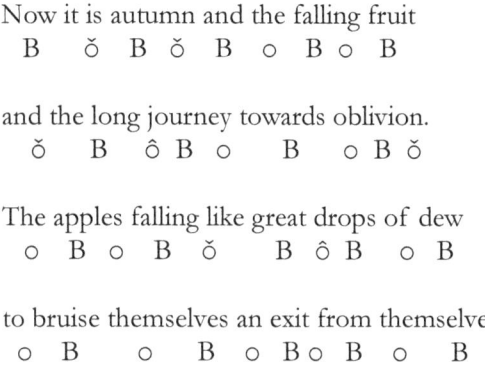

Now it is autumn and the falling fruit
  B   ŏ B ŏ B o B o B

and the long journey towards oblivion.
  ŏ   B   ô B o   B   o B ŏ

The apples falling like great drops of dew
  o   B o B ŏ   B ô B   o B

to bruise themselves an exit from themselves
  o B   o   B o B o B o   B

from "The Ship of Death", D. H. Lawrence (1929)

APPENDIX II
A FEW ADDITIONAL "SEMI-FORMAL" CONTEMPORARY POEMS:

Allen, Dick: "Veteran's Day"
Alvarez, Julia: "Sonnet I"
Dove, Rita: "Parsley"
Ewart, Gavin: "The Last Things"
Glück, Louise: "Bridal Piece"
Gorham, Sarah: "The White Tiger Leaps"
Heffernan, Michael: "A Colloquy of Silences"
Jenkins, Alan: "Murphy's Law"
Klappert, Peter: "Ellie Mae Leaves in a Hurry"
Meinke, Peter: "Rage"
Wojahn, David: "The Assassination of John Lennon as Depicted by the Madame Tussaud Wax Museum, Niagara Falls, Ontario, 1987"

Steven Winn

Postres

—From the dessert card at La Provença, Barcelona

The meal is something to be gotten through,
a sturdy litany of bream and hake
and turbot swathed in Pernod. There's kangaroo
and pork and entrecote and oxtail baked
until it oozes marrow on the plate.

The salads, half-forgotten in the press
of sauces primed with raisins, nuts or leeks,
strike first. The bristling, gaudy greens are dressed
and gleam in oil and balsamic sheets
that loll across the tongue until the sweets.

It's then, the table crumbed and starkly bare
as if to banish baser appetite,
that coy mischief and seduction share
attention in the second menu's flights
of yogurt mousse with wild fruits, a light

unlikely soup (with lemon jelly) made
of melon and tomato. Chocolate comes
tri-textured and presented à la mode
with mild-oil ice cream. Champagne foams
over some other fruits. Our choices roam

from this to that—and what about that creamy
saffron with its precious melon pearls? At last
we settle. In truth, it almost seems unseemly
to continue. We're full. Oh, we'll fast
at home. What comes after is what lasts.

Ted Mc Carthy

Nearly

Too soon to wake, too late to welcome sleep,
I fight what's become a nightly war with stillness,
a waning moon's imprint on threadbare drapes
weak as a fading memory of wholeness;
I picture you today, all skin and bone,
your dinner of Red Bull and Mayfair Blue,
your shoulders tautened by a whirring brain
that spins a shadow of the girl I knew:
and all that pain no makeover can dull,
that word you still can't bring yourself to say
except as xxx or lol.
Strange how the simplest things are bought so dearly.
I think of you asleep, your dream of clay,
and all that beauty, not quite lost, but nearly.

Rebecca Foust

The Speaker Tries Medication

Underneath all that irony and hoped-for wit
there was something not all that funny,
something sort of sad. Like that sign
she'd seen in the Tenderloin,
Syringes "R" Us. A real gut-buster.
At first. And then. And then. And then not.
Lately it was more often not
than not, and she'd gotten fed up with Bleak.
She was hormonal and had bad moods. Oh shit,
just say it, she was sad. S-A-D, sad.
Prozac helped until she got numb
to being numb all the time, and the pain
came back. *Ashes, ashes we all fall down.*
Same old plague. Just a new, improved strain.

David Alpaugh

Richard Cory (His Untold Story)

Turns out Richard Cory had pancreatic cancer;
Was told he had, at best, six months to live.
After the initial shock, he called his lawyer
To help draw up the will in which he'd give

The wealth so many envied mostly to charity;
His custom-tailored suits to Salvation Army.
Probate only noticed one peculiarity:
That provision for his cat! Was Cory *barmy*?

No one but his doctor knew what was going on.
There was no one on the pavement he could tell.
His friends were fair-weather; parents long gone;
Glib *how are yous* were answered with *I'm well*.

The pain finally got so bad he couldn't walk
Downtown; couldn't even climb out of bed.
You can guess the rest. To hell with idle talk
As to why Dick put that bullet through his head.

FEATURED ARTIST

Massimo Sbreni
A Photographic Exhibit

Massimo Sbreni is an inspired people and travel photographer from Ravenna, Italy. His photography portrays faces and acts of the distant worlds, capturing the souls of the places he visits while often emphasizing the human figure and way of life.

Travel Photojournalism Flickr Group notes:

> His images have been mainly captured during the numerous trips that he has had the opportunity to take, especially in Asia. He loves street photography and portraiture. He is very interested in using photography to capture emotion, which can then be emphasized, blunted or even distorted through his choice of composition and post-processing. He works in both color and black and white, and despite mixing the two media, his style remains remarkably consistent. His dream is to be able to work and live through photography. At this time, he does not consider himself a professional.

★ ★ ★

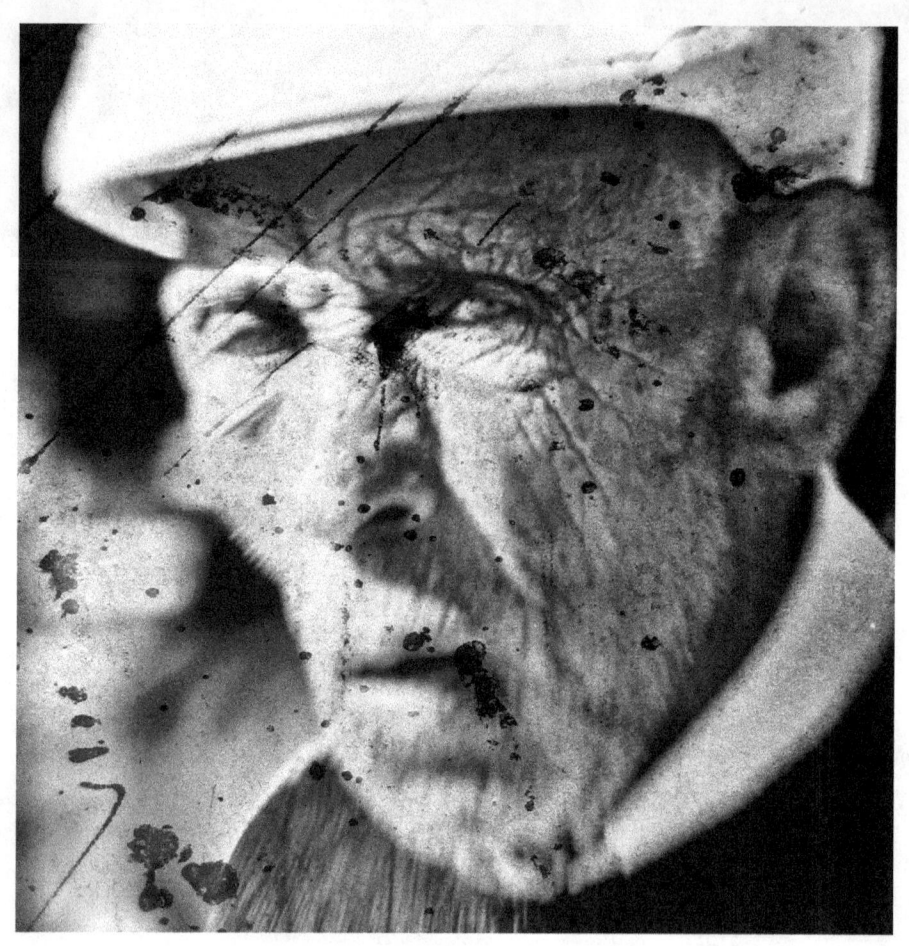

MEMOIR

Steve Bucknell
The Mystery of R.P. Lister

First Encounter

I first encounter R.P. Lister as I leaf through a second-hand copy of the 1978 *New Oxford Book of Light Verse* edited by Kingsley Amis. I read *The Revolutionaries* and *The Idle Demon*, two sharp and witty verses of his and begin to wonder who this writer is. My curiosity leads me to start looking for traces of Lister on the Internet. I am intrigued by the little information I find there: facts such as, he is Richard Percival Lister, born in 1914, a Fellow of the Royal Society of Literature and has published poems in *Punch* and *The New Yorker*. But that is all. I find no obituary, so I begin to wonder all the more what has become of him and his work.

Beginning the Quest

I like the poems so much that I quote one in contribution to a playful thread posted on the *Eratosphere* site and I begin to record my search in a thread, hoping that others will join me in looking for R.P.L., as I begin to think of him. Others do find and post poems, and seem to share my excitement at discovering this clever, wistful and funny poet.

I make a first breakthrough, finding in the on-line archives of the British Library a catalogue of 21 works by R.P.L. From Amazon I order a copy of his book *The Questing Beast* and a copy of *The Idle Demon*. *The Questing Beast* turns out to be a stunningly good novel. I am in awe of his liveliness, wit and his stylish writing. I hope others will get interested and seek out the works of this writer.

The Idle Demon arrives full of treasures originally published in *Punch*, *The Atlantic Monthly* and *The New Yorker*. Once again, frustratingly, there is no biographical information. On the back of the dust-jacket, he is listed with Stevie Smith, Roy Fuller, David Wright, Laurie Lee, Elizabeth Jennings, David Gascoyne and H.D., all Deutsch authors of whom I have heard, have read. Why has Lister disappeared? Was he considered lightweight, old-fashioned, formalist? Where did he fit in to the literary world of the time? His work still seems fresh and funny to me, underpinned by a depth of feeling.

I head deeper into the mystery; I make plans to visit the British Library to look at some of his books in the hope of gleaning more biographical background. The catalogue doesn't make it clear what many of his works are. *The Idle Demon* is recorded as a collection of verses, published by Andre Deutsch in London in 1958, but other works aren't identified as clearly. Are they novels, poems, travel books or something else? To further my researches, I sign on through the Internet as a temporary reader at the British Library, and order three books to be available for my visit.

Almost a Conversation

I enjoy my initiation into the British Library. I sign in at the registration desk. No coats, no bags except clear plastic, no sharp objects . . . no pens allowed! I have to go and buy myself a pencil from the shop. Then I have my photo taken (I look smug and beardy and pleased with myself) and they give me my Reader's card. "Researching The World's Knowledge", it says on the plastic card.

The most interesting book I find turns out to be *Me and the Holy Spirit*, 1999, published by Pauline Dorricott Books. It is A4 in format and looks like a self-published book, which explains why I could find no trace of Pauline Dorricott as a publisher on the Internet. The book is a humorous meditation on the Trinity, and why R.P.L. prefers the Holy Ghost to the other two. He likes the way all it seems to do is sometimes fill people—or sometimes not. Yet he feels that it is "some pervasive influence in the universe."

The book tells me how he felt in 1999. He asks himself at one point: "What is left to me?" He answers:

> Reasonably good health at an enormous age; dozens of loving friends; a love of music in an age when it is on tap in the home at all hours; a taste for writing and painting and the ability to make a small but sufficient living if necessary; a small and unexpected legacy making it unnecessary to make a living at either, so that I can do both simply for fun; an agreeable, if rather small flat in W11 fifteen minutes walk from the park. Few princes can have had so much to enjoy and so little to fear or resent.
> —from *Me and the Holy Spirit*

He describes how although he made a living as a writer up to the 1980s he was "never part of a Circle", and feels that it has been this "lack of Circularity" that has seen his reputation fade away. I read on, totally absorbed, thinking of how he described the character Pellinew in *The Questing Beast*,

> Talking to Pellinew, you sometimes forgot that the world was real, and that its needs, in the way of rent or food, had to be attended to.

I can imagine the friends of R.P.L. feeling the same way. I feel the same way surrounded by the purposeful hush of the great library. I look up for the first time and find a dark-haired girl scribbling at the next table. I ask to borrow her pencil-sharpener and she whispers, "Yes." Sharpened, I continue to pencil more of R.P.L.'s words. It feels as if he is talking to me: "about the age fifty-five, when times were really rather hard, I decided that the only way of coping with life was to accept (as gladly as I could manage) what was sent and make the best of it. And this principle has served me so well that I am in no mind to abandon it." I realize that I will be fifty-five in November this year, a day before R.P.L. turns ninety-six.

Our "conversation" continues through the afternoon. I learn more about his life. His first marriage failed early on, but then from the age of seventy to seventy-four he married again and had "four very happy years" with Ione. Then, tragically, Ione died of cancer leaving R.P.L. without a partner again. He laments that he has spent a greater part of his life without this close companionship and love. He writes movingly in *The Questing Beast*: "When you are possessed by a longing for someone in this way, the whole of life relates itself to that one, important thing. Then, in the course of time, the feeling dies away, and you can no longer recapture the greatness and reality of it."

At the end of *Me and the Holy Spirit*, he says that if there is a heaven he will not be "one of the saints" who go marching in. I feel sure that he would be among the princes, and that his princess, Ione, will be there waiting impatiently for him. The afternoon in the British Library makes me feel as if I have been deep in conversation with Richard Lister. He even confides in me the meaning of life. What is it?

> It has none. Not of itself. You put your own meaning into it; and that is its meaning. Or if you say it is meaningless, so it is.
> —from *Me and the Holy Spirit*

The Phone Call

The next breakthrough comes when my wife posts a question on the BBC *The Archers* message board, asking for any information on R.P.L. Someone points us to the *International Who's Who of Writers*. This has a small amount of biographical information. And an address.... It might be possible to contact him, even visit him. Of course, I realize I should not rush in: he might not be well, I might not be wanted. I email and ask if it might be possible to get in touch.

A couple of days later the telephone rings and someone says, "Hello, this is Richard." He is phoning me out of the blue. My email must have prompted someone to give him my number. I spend an hour chatting to him. I discover that his health remains excellent and his mind remains sharp.

Coincidence piles on coincidence. Before the Second World War he worked as a metallurgist at Samuel Fox's steelworks near Sheffield, not far from where we live. He lodged at a farmhouse in Upper Midhope. He has walked the same walks, been to the same pubs and enjoyed this landscape of moors and reservoirs. He worked in his protected profession through the war in London at the Ministry of Aircraft Production, experiencing the Blitz. After the war he made a decent living from writing, and gave up working as a metallurgist. He rates the poems he placed in *The Atlantic Monthly* as some of his best. He thinks *The Idle Demon* is his best collection of verse.

I find out that he was a friend of Graham Greene, through the latter's publisher wife, Elaine Greene. He describes Greene as "a very nice man, very approachable." He confirms that he didn't really mix in literary circles or read much contemporary poetry, but he admired T.S. Eliot and Dylan Thomas. His great love was travel. He says his book on Turkey is "O.K. as a guide", but recommends his *Journey in Lapland* which he says is much more personal, and is also the account of a great love affair with an American woman called Carla, who returned to California, after two months spent walking with him.

He is as curious about me as I have been about him. We exchange cat stories, we discuss psychiatry. I remind him of his very skeptical take on 'trick-cyclists' in *The Questing Beast*. That was just the character, he says; he himself felt that a psychiatrist he had known had helped him greatly in his younger days. He is pleased that I have "a proper job" as a mental health nurse. There is so much I want to know. He still loves music. He loves Mozart and Wagner, and Elgar, Britten and Vaughan Williams.

I tell him that I have posted poems of his on the *Eratosphere* site. He is pleased about this, and interested to know that his books are still available through Amazon, but I get the impression that he is unfamiliar with the Internet. He is pleased that people are discussing and enjoying his work. At the end of the conversation I write on the *Eratosphere* thread:

> I have Richard's phone number, I have his address. I am honored and amazed. I will hear his warm chuckling, his descriptions of his "very lucky" life in my head for a long time. At the end I asked the usual, boring question about his longevity. "Oh that," he said. "Walking, lots of walking. Come down; come down for a chat and a drink!"

We Arrange to Meet

A week or so later, I ring Richard back and tell him how much I have enjoyed reading *The Questing Beast* on holiday, and how much my wife Adrienne has enjoyed it too. Like me she was laughing out loud at his typical sharpness and wit. It's excellent about life in wartime, about psychiatry and the search for love and meaning. Adrienne has pointed out parallels between it and Rose Macaulay's *The Towers of Trebizond*. Richard agrees, and says he loved her work, and the paths of their travels seem to have crossed, though they never met. He has vivid memories of Trebizond in Turkey, and tells me, "You must go."

I pass on the pleasure people on *Eratosphere* have expressed in discovering his poems. He really thinks this is wonderful; he thought they had all been forgotten. I arrange to meet Richard at his home in London in a month's time. I pass on that people on the *Eratosphere* are rediscovering and enjoying *The Idle Demon*.

My Meeting with Richard

I feel like the questing beast as I make my way down to London to meet Richard Percival Lister for the first time. In one version of the legend, the patchwork beast pines for the chivalric knight who has grown too ancient to hunt him, and so sets off in search of him.

I enter the Underground labyrinth warily, crossing London and change lines at Oxford Circus. The warning "Serious Delays Expected" on the Victoria line alarms me, but I wait patiently and the first tube train rushes in. I visit London rarely, but since the bombs of 2005 I'm sure something has changed. People on the Tube are more aware of each other, conscious of proximity and dependence. I notice people offer their seats to others who might be in more need and people talk a little more. There is a sense of shared frailty and togetherness.

Without incident, I emerge at Holland Park. Adrienne has led me through a Google Street View of the route I must take, so everything looks familiar. I get the odd sensation of this being the way home. I stop for a bottle of wine at an off-license I know will be there. At the top of the street, I spot an emissary looking out for me. This must be Meg, Richard's good friend and support, who helped organize our meeting. I plant a kiss on her surprised cheek before she has time to say hello. She tells me Richard has been getting impatient.

As we enter the door of his flat, Richard launches his tall, unsteady self into the air to grasp my hand and welcome me. I know him at once from the likeness captured by the Elena Jahn Clough drawing on the back cover of *A Journey in Lapland*. He has a Sherlock Holmes-like mien, with added wit and charm.

Meg organizes us, sits us down, feeds us delicacies and opens the wine. The small sitting room is full of light. I am conscious of Richard's own jewel-like paintings on the walls, of books, of the piano at my arm with music from Bach and Beethoven resting on it. I am not at a loss, as I feared I might be, but talk too much, trying to give Richard some sense of what his writing means to me, and how others on the *Eratosphere* site are enjoying his work. He chuckles indulgently and surprises Meg by fluently quoting his own poetry back to me.

I tell him of the emblematic importance his poem *Ballade on Experience* has for me. Its refrain: "Everything has not happened to me yet" has become a guide. When I recall its last stanza I think of our meeting:

> Most noble Prince, empanoplied and spurred,
> Do not despair because we have not met;
> Although my back is bent, my vision blurred,
> Everything has not happened to me yet.

We spend the next hour enjoying a heady ping-pong of lines from Richard's poems. I tease him about his "genius", and he acknowledges and accepts the appellation. We read his "Genius Defined" from *The Idle Demon*.

> Genius is a common factor found
> In many widely different kinds of man,
> As, for example, Plato, Petrarch, Pound,
> Cervantes, Caesar, Socrates, Cézanne,
>
> Marlborough, Milton, Mendelssohn, Mozart,
> Puccini, Pushkin, Proust, Picasso, Poe,
> Beethoven, Botticelli, Bonaparte,
> Mohammed, Mendel, Michelangelo,
>
> El Greco, Gorki, Gaugin, Goethe, Grock,
> Defoe, Debussy, Darwin, Dante, Drake,
> Canova, Casanova, Caradoc,
> Bach, Belisarius, Bunyan, Buddha, Blake,
>
> Tolstoy, Tertullian, Turner, Trumper, Tree,
> Machiavelli, Molière, and me.

We laugh a lot. We talk about Time, which is one of the great themes of his poetry. I read his *Tarry Awhile Time* to him and Meg. It has rich echoes of Marvell and Rochester for me. Richard loves Shakespeare, the Metaphysicals, and the Classics. His grandfather passed on to him a depth of reading and a love of literature. I get the impression that, like me, Richard is mostly self-taught in literature. Unlike me, he is a self-taught linguist. He loves Dante and playfully recites the first Canto of *The Divine Comedy* to entertain us. I quiz him on some Kafka-like echoes I had caught in his novel, *The Way Backwards*. "Yes," he says. Of course, he was reading Kafka in German at the time.

He talks about his visits to America, staying in Arizona and Michigan with friends. He has fond memories of New York and of publishing his poems in *The New Yorker* and spending many convivial evenings with its poetry editor, Howard Moss, in Greenwich Village. When I ask Richard to recommend his best novel, he tells me "Ah, that will be *The Covered City*, an unpublished novel of mine." This sounds fascinating: a novel set in a future when London is roofed over, and on that roof another city grows. "Not Science Fiction," Richard quickly says, "a novel about people." At the time, publishers said it was too long, but when he cut it down it lost too much. Later on, I see this large pale-blue manuscript sitting on a shelf in Richard's bedroom. As Richard says, some of his unpublished, uncollected works "still haunt me." It makes me hope that I can play a part in bringing Richard's writings into the public eye again.

Richard continues to write poetry, although his main endeavor from about 1980 has been painting. He writes in the introduction to *Nine Legends*: "In 1980 people started buying my paintings, so I took to painting in all the time I had available to me. Painting from then on occupied me happily and kept me alive for the next ten years." He quotes Cézanne and Van Gogh as influences on his own art. His sense of color is strong; some of the landscapes, almost abstract, remind me of Paul Klee. The sense of enjoyment and pleasure in life shines through these paintings as it does through his writing. No wonder they sold well.

Through his shared interest in painting with Meg, Richard has enjoyed many painting, walking and writing holidays at Bussas in France. He also still actively pursues his love of music: attending concerts and the ballet in London with Meg and friends. As someone wrote in a scrapbook of tributes for his 90th birthday, he truly is "a Renaissance Man".

It has been a life-affirming experience for me to meet Richard. He gives me a sense that all is still possible. He believes in life, and gets such pleasure from life while acknowledging its frailty. Like all of us he admits to feeling "low in the water" at times, yet his poems seduce and outwit time. He is indeed a gentle Knight and Troubadour. What does age matter? I quote the last two stanzas of "The Troubadour" from *The Idle Demon*:

> His bones seek their Jerusalem; and mine
> Creep yet another stage
> By song and tourney and the crimson wine
> Towards old age.
>
> But age, for troubadours? A song not sung
> Haunts me again, as in the straw I lie,
> Knowing the world still young, myself still young,
> And all Provence, and its wide sky.

I depart later that day bearing signed copies, carrying unpublished poems, happy to have met such a remarkable man. Richard remains frail, as we all are, but this "frailty" has lasted him for many years, and I hope for many more years to come. He is surrounded by loving friends and family, by Meg and her family, and by his books and music. As I am leaving I spot *The Rings of Saturn* by W.G. Sebald—a fellow-walker, thinker and writer—lying on a shelf. Richard is still reading, still writing, still keeping up-to-date. As I sit on the train back to Sheffield, I recall his tall figure at the door of his flat, waving to me as I leave. I leave thinking, again, of Richard's *Ballade on Experience*: "Everything has not happened to [us] yet."

FEATURED POET

Richard Percival Lister
Interviewed by Steve Bucknell

Richard Percival Lister was born in Nottingham in 1914. His childhood was spent in West Didsbury, and in the Peak District of Derbyshire. After school in New Mills, he studied at Manchester University, graduating with a BSc in Metallurgy. He worked as a metallurgist in Sheffield before the Second World War, and then at the Royal Naval Torpedo Factory in Greenock in Scotland, the Royal Aircraft Establishment in Farnborough, and the Ministry of Aircraft Production in London. After an earlier marriage to Joyce Ambler, he married Ione Mary Wynniatt Husey in 1985, a very happy marriage until her death in 1989.

He became a full-time writer in 1950. He published over 400 poems, many in *Punch*, *The New Yorker* and *The Atlantic Monthly*. His collection of verse *The Idle Demon* was published in 1958 by Deutsch in the UK, and Macmillan in the USA. He published six novels, two travel books, and biographical works on Genghis Khan, Marco Polo and Herodotus. He became a Fellow of the Royal Society of Literature in 1970. From 1975, though painting became his main source of income, he continued to write stories and lyrical verse, maintaining his lifelong interest in literature, music and the arts. He reads German, Italian, French, and some Spanish, and quotes as influences on his work Heine, Dante, the French troubadour tradition, and G.K. Chesterton.

★ ★ ★

Steve: When we first met, you said your grandfather was a big influence on you becoming a poet. Can you tell me about the influence he had?

Richard: My grandfather was a very-well read and learned man. He was a Methodist minister, with a very good classical background. He had an MA from Edinburgh University, and knew nine languages. He spoke to me about many subjects, including literature and the arts. He opened my mind on many subjects about which I later felt compelled to write.

When we used to visit him, when we were small, my brother and I played on a typewriter he owned, and he encouraged me to write. He always took an interest in what I was writing.

What influences did your parents have?

No influence at all on what I wrote, but my father was very encouraging and interested in my poetry and kept a file of his own of all my poems. My mother passed on to me a love of music and taught me to play the piano.

You trained and worked as a metallurgist in the 1930s and during the Second World War. How did you happen to become a poet and novelist given this background?

I always thought of myself as a poet. I wrote my first poem when I was six, when I heard about Lord Carnarvon discovering the tomb of Tutankhamen. This was it:

> Lord Carnarvon loved to work.
> He said he did, you know,
> He raked the garden with a rake
> And hoed it with a hoe.

Although I was a metallurgist by profession I always wrote poems for pleasure. They came into my head and I had to write them down! I like writing novels, but poetry is what I just do. I started sending poems to *Punch* in the 1940s and had some published. My first wife, Joyce, took some poems to be typed out in a typing agency in Wigmore Street, and the person who ran the bureau told her about a group of writers called The Saturdays, which I joined. We met each week. A subject would be picked from a hat and we would each write a poem in fifteen minutes. Each of us had our own "Grey Book" of poems or ideas for poems.

Later on, I sent some of my work to Siegfried Sassoon, whom I much admired. I like the way his poetry can be satirical. I asked him if he thought they were worth anything, and he wrote back saying "I think they are well crafted and you should publish", which was a tremendous encouragement.

As time went on, I was making an income from the poems in *Punch*, and in *The New Yorker* and *Atlantic Monthly*, and I needed lots of time for writing, so I gave up the job as a metallurgist, so I could work on my novels and poetry. *Punch* paid reasonably well, and I was producing plenty of poems. At that time *Punch* was a magazine with a mass circulation. My grandfather always took *Punch*, as did other families.

Did you get a lot of feedback on your work?

Not in Britain, there was very little—I think that's how we are. However, I got a lot of correspondence from the States, about poems in *The New Yorker* and *Atlantic Monthly*. In fact, when I went to the States in 1962 or 1963, I knew a lot of people from the correspondence, and made some friends, who I went to stay with, all over the place. When I was in New York, I used to spend time with Howard Moss, the poetry editor of *The New Yorker*. I liked Howard Moss very much. He was a good poet, a great editor and a terribly nice man.

You were quite active at one time, writing and publishing regularly up till 1980. Why did you stop for so long?

I went on publishing my work until 1975 (when I was 65) but continued to write poetry. I did some proofreading, editing and painting, and together these gave me a reasonable income. I became more interested in painting, and had several one-man shows in London. However, I continued to write poetry.

You started writing at a time when free verse was becoming the dominant mode of writing for most poets. Why did you always write formal verse? And how did this help or hinder your writing?

I automatically think of poetry being rhythmical and rhyming and that was what I felt comfortable with. I think I was influenced by the poetry I first read and heard and by the poetry I studied at school, such as Wordsworth, Tennyson, and Shakespeare. Writing poetry that rhymed and scanned probably affected my poetry career as my work became no longer fashionable. This is why my poems appeared mainly, not in literary magazines, but rather as witty poetry in publications such as *Punch*, *The New Yorker* and the *Atlantic Monthly* of Boston; I am still a Fellow of The Royal Society of Literature, but otherwise I am little known!

Who are some of your favorite poets and writers? And who do you think influenced your writing?

From when I was young, I think I was influenced by Edward Lear and Lewis Carroll. The first book I owned was by Lewis Carroll. My mother gave my brother a copy of *Alice in Wonderland*, and gave me a copy of *Through the Looking Glass*. Carroll was a very modern author, before his time, I think. I was influenced a lot by G.K. Chesterton, and his poems are some of my favorites. I gave a lecture to the Royal Society of Literature on them once. I also like Omar Khayyam. And of course I looked up to T.S. Eliot, and liked the poetry of Dylan Thomas. I rarely read modern poetry.

I think *King Lear* is my favorite Shakespeare play—very dark, a brutal play. I learned French and German, whilst at University, and I like Heine very much—you should learn German, Steve, to read Heine in the original. I learned Italian to read Dante, and can now read Italian for pleasure. I really like Natalia Ginzburg. She writes in Italian, a marvelous short story writer, she is a lovely writer, lovely use of humor. I did learn Spanish so I could read Cervantes' *Don Quixote* in the original, which I enjoyed, and I also liked Marquez's *One Hundred Years of Solitude*—have you read it? It's terrific. Of the people who were writing when I was being published, I liked Christopher Isherwood, and I enjoyed Graham Greene's works, and Aldous Huxley.

What about the French troubadour tradition? This seems to be a theme or influence you return to from time to time in your work?

Yes, I wrote a poem in the *Idle Demon*—"The Troubadour"—"A song not sung / Haunts me again as in the straw I lie." I tried to learn Old French to read some of the work, but it wasn't easy. I am keen on the idea of Troubadours though, going round the country, strumming and singing, and sleeping in the fields under the sky of Provence.

Of all the poems you've written, is there one that stands out for you as your most satisfying?

There are several I like. "Griffin" is very autobiographical. I was alone and didn't belong—but I don't feel that now. "The Gardens of the Morning" reminds me of my childhood. I like "The Lament of an Idle Demon"; and "The Field of Dynamite" and "Freedom's Mansion" are big favorites. I also like "The Owlet and the Gamekeeper", "Before the Ball", "The Stars Spirits of my Ancestors"—oh yes, and "My Heart is Like an Onion". These are all from *The Idle Demon*.

And from *The Albatross*, I like "On Being Born in the Wrong Age".

What are your ambitions for your work in the future?

I'd like lots of people to read it and enjoy it.

I would like to see a *Collected Poems*. Yes, that's number one ambition! A lot were published in the magazines—it would be nice to have another collection. . . .

Yes, that would be wonderful! Thank you, Richard, for making me welcome and sharing your thoughts with us.

Featured Poetry
New Poems from R.P. Lister
* * *

R.P. Lister

The Length of Time

The length of time is like a piece of string.
It may be long, or short, or anything.
It comes and goes, and varies with the day;
It starts and stops, and flags, and fades away.

Sometimes it has no breadth, sometimes no height.
It grasps the day, and turns it into night.
It twists and turns, and wriggles like a snake;
It may be half asleep or wide awake.

Such is the length of time, and such its habits.
Its inconsistency is like a rabbit's;
It comes and goes, and dives into a hole.
It is a home for the immortal soul
Which flaps and fiddles between joy and sorrow,
Which lives for evermore, but dies tomorrow.

The length of time is an eternal riddle,
Which has two ends, but nothing in the middle.
You can take time, and you can beat it;
You can do time, waste it, or fleet it,
But you can't eat it.

—*May 1997*

R.P. Lister

Darling Death

    Come and get me, darling Death,
        But not yet:
    There's a lot worth living for.
        So don't forget
    To wait until I've drawn my very final breath.

    And even then I might have more
    To say or do before I go.
          So
      Be reasonably slow;

      To be in haste
    Would be in the very worst of taste.
    There's a great deal I have to do;
    Some of it old, some of it new.
    Some tales to tell, some pots to glue.

    And even then there might be more to come.
        "O the brave music of a distant drum!"

—October 2007

R.P. Lister

The Haunted

Behold the hideous hosts,
The inharmonious and the hated.
But there are friendlier ghosts,
That comfort when cultivated.

There is no real harm in the toffee-nosed,
    Once out of sight;
    They can be redecomposed
And redeclassified as trite.

I hear a blackbird singing
From the very depths of his song;
And the beneficent benedictions of his bringing
    Will not be lost on us for long.

R.P. Lister

Infected Eyes

Infected eyes—rose red are they
And glow at night when all is dark.
The little children run away,
The dogs bark,
The populace takes refuge in the Park.

There was a time when both those eyes were blue
And shone at night with a refulgent beam
That now is of a red and violent hue.
Old ladies faint, and little children scream.
Everyone cries;
Take, take away those red, red eyes!

—October 2007

R.P. Lister

Stardust

Such is the dust of stars that fills the skies
It is a wonder we can see at all.
There is a mist, a fog, a murky pall
Eternally suspended curtainwise
Before our baffled and enquiring eyes.
If we could only pierce that foggy wall

We might perceive some fragments of the truth
Lying dispersed like diamonds in a midden.
Even the smallest fragment, though, is hidden.
The human race is in its earliest youth,

And so I cannot see the wood for the trees.
    Stardust, stardust is all it sees.

—May 1997

R.P. Lister

The Slow Loris

Inch by slow inch the loris crawls
Toward some goal, some goal that calls
With such persistence that he falls
Into no chasm: never walls
Impede him: never crag appalls.

Such is the prey of great Desire
That fears no flood and flees no fire,
Yields to no plea, shrinks from no ire.
Derides despair; he does not tire,
Nor even dreads the funeral pyre.

Wholly along predestined grooves
He slowly, slowly, slowly moves.

—*May 1997*

R.P. Lister

The Stork

The stork brings babies
And hangs them in the trees.
Some get rabies
From transitory bees.

But others are collected
By mothers passing by.
Some get quite dejected
While hanging in the sky.

And, growing up, remember
Even when they are old,
The bare trees in December,
The rain, the wind, the cold.

—May 2000

R.P. Lister

Nokia

Who's a Nokia on my door
What she going Nokia for
One, two, three, wait for me
Don't go Nokia any more

Nokia, Nokia, who's there
Who's a sitting in my chair
Four, five, six, picking up sticks
People Nokia everywhere

Nokia up, Nokia down,
Things go Nokia all over the town
Wherever I go I always shout
One more Nokia and you're out!

Nokia on, Nokia off
Wherever I go they always scoff
You could Nokia if you could
Always Nokia on wood

Nokia out, Nokia in
Knock me down with a safety pin
Nokia, Nokia, three by three
That will be quite enough for me

—*January 2008*

R.P. Lister

To Be Alive

Sometime this year I shall be 95
And still it is a joy to be alive!
To walk, to talk, to think, to drink, to sneeze,
Is there, my friends, a greater joy than these?
Sit by me, I will tell you all a tale.
There is, my friends, one joy that does not fail.
It is no sin, it asks for no forgiving.
It simply is the simple joy of living.
One may be tired or hungry or in debt,
And yet, my friends, do not forget
That whether we falter, fail or thrive
It is a privilege to be alive.
Do not be sad, rather raise a cheer
For the peculiar fact that we are here.
There is still time to laugh or cry in
And there is all infinity to die in!

—March 2009

Gail White

A Crisis in Mesa Verde

The gatherers have gone away,
picked up their baskets and departed.
Hunters huddle in dismay.
The gatherers have gone away,
just leaving bread for one more day.
No hearth is swept, no fire started.
The gatherers have gone away,
picked up their baskets and departed.

The hunters put aside their spears
and look around them, disbelieving.
Gatherers fed the tribe for years.
The hunters lay aside their spears
and try to calm the children's fears
while wondering who will do the weaving.
Hunters put aside their spears
and look around them, disbelieving.

Slowly the pile of bones will rise,
the children drift away unheeded.
Could it have happened otherwise?
Slowly the pile of bones will rise,
the clothes wear out, the vats draw flies.
The hot clay ovens won't be needed.
Slowly the pile of bones will rise,
the children drift away unheeded.

No one will know in years to come
what happened here in bygone ages.
The land that knew them will be dumb.
No one will know in years to come
if death came soon and found them numb
or took them off in easy stages.
No one will know in years to come
what happened here in bygone ages.

J. Patrick Lewis

At the Hotel Ukrainya
A Century Ago

—1973

The *dezhurnaya* hands me the key
to my room in the Ukraine Hotel.
Her marble eye conjures a spell
for a fool of a foreigner like me,
unaware he's surrounded by strange
walls wired to the telephone exchange.

The radio over the bed
plays round-the-clock static to Stalin,
whose twenty-year phantom has fallen
ass over teacup on his head,
a fact that's as obvious to note
as it is suicidal to quote.

On Kutuzovsky Prospekt, two big,
greatcoat policemen detain
a *tovarich*, coarse, loud, vodka-veined,
and hustle the lout to the brig,
while cars on the boulevard slow
in the comforting safety of snow.

I lie here where dead men once lay,
a conspirator's cradle of lies,
where dour *apparatchiks* and spies,
ever minding their roles in a play,
could not apprehend the idea
that evil was no panacea.

Frank Osen

Ligan

> *such a parcell of goods as the Mariners in a danger of shipwracke cast out . . . and fasten to them a boigh . . . that so they may find them, and have them againe . . . are called . . . ligan*
> —Les Termes de la Ley (1636), p. 446.

A storm can wrack or rocks may rend,
and sometimes, crueler calms rescind
the quick directives of the wind;
a momentary tide can blend

and swallow all the evidence,
so finding the knotted line, the barrel,
they'd only have the helpless sense
she was, and knew she was, in peril.

Though terrified she'd sink or burn,
her hands made fast and cast adrift,
buoyant, blazoned as a gift,
this surety of safe return.

Some people on the peaceful quay
make light about the ends of rope,
but should you founder on the sea,
know—it's marked and harbored hope.

Wendy Videlock

Debrief

The rains finally came,
in sacks of sugar, rice,
and grain. Another sign

arrived by slow, slow train.
She possessed the voice of a loon,
lips like snow, and a shock

of dark hair below. Elsewhere,
Viking ships and long hymns
reflect six-pointed stars

and the promise of another shore.
I have seen two copper coins
and an urn of dust presented as

a means of passage.
A tiny pearl is placed in
the belly of a bowl. One great light

commences at the tail
of every dark night.
The locals do not find this strange.

They often speak of time
as the animal which takes flight,
stands still, and in the face

of travel, bends.
This is not evidence
of gods and goddesses,

my friends. I bring with me
no evidence or proof of the soul.
These events from the surface

of the blue-throated bird
are mere suggestions. The merest
suggestions of another world.

Wendy Videlock

Dear Moon,

Is there such a thing
as passive

verb, the first

word,

the great
pearl,

the mute
bird,

or separating heart
from wild, signed

a very small
child

Wendy Videlock

In Beth's Garden

Poplars, firs,
hollyhocks,
barrels and barrels

of apricots,
arches, asters,

desert stone,
of sweet

tobacco
she rolls her own,
adobe, pantry,

spiral stairs,

easels, bees,
many chairs,

sorrow's waters,

painted pears,
moons,

mums,

the lyric air.

Ned Balbo

Marco Polo Collects Bird Eggs

—After Nora Sturges' painting

It's crucial to be patient, delicate.
Your rolling cart is jammed with specimens
boxed up or caged: goldfinch, exotic bluebird
singing in their shared sorrow; yellow gourds,

long sea-green seed-pods, parked in morning light.
A skunk, too—crucial to be delicate!—
and yet, there's more to find along this detour
that has left you reeling. The cliffs you've reached—

sheer walls of smooth rock, grass-edged, pocked with shrubs—
are home to species few have ever seen,
and patience is rewarded. . . . Delicate
in blue gloves, on your stomach you reach out

for rare eggs in an aerie, speckled shells
you'll grasp, possess, and incubate. Then—what?
You'll find the downy hatchling in your hands,
famished, requires some crucial delicacy

you haven't got or no one knows exists.
—Banish the thought! The houses huddled near,
held hostage to such heights, unlatch green doors
to greet those gorgeous wings above the gorge

that dive toward nests you must not desecrate.

Leslie Monsour

In Such a Place

I'm killing minutes in a city park,
Reflecting while the sky turns overcast.
Strange how the orderly, unblemished grounds
Appear to have no vestige of the past.

The parking meters accept credit cards.
The shrubbery is plain and well-behaved.
Two ravens poke the lawn half-heartedly.
The spaces in between the grass are paved.

Birdsong is banished by the leaf blower
and power mower edging ficus trunks.
The gas fumes are the only vagrants here,
Loitering in the air like drowsy drunks.

A man who walks a Yorkie on a leash
Pauses to let the tiny dog complete
A tiny crap, dispatched with plastic bag,
And carried to a bin across the street.

There's no dead branch in sight, no memory;
No process of decay, nothing to burn.
Where nothing rots, nothing surprising lives.
In such a place, what more is there to learn?

John Beaton

To the Dead of Winter

— *Little Qualicum River, after the fall salmon run*

Now is the time of the moss
and it blankets the alders en masse
as they stand in the mists of the bottomland;
though witch's hair drapes from their frames
they're but haggard old widows in weeds
who abide by the graves of your race,
      for these trees seem so sere that their sap will not rise,
      that their laceworks of leaves will not lattice the skies
      though their grayness and gauntness have donned the disguise
of these snow-sprinkled greensleeves of fleece.

Now is the time of the snow
though at noon there's a moment of thaw
when the river runs clear by the skulls
and the gill-plates at rest in the shallows
or enveloped in white on the gravel
like masks. And your head has a jaw
      that grew hooked as you ran with your instincts aflame
      and your scales turning scarlet; the maples became
      inflamed with your fire which the winter would tame
as it laid down your dead like the law.

Now is the time of the dead
between fall, when the fleshpots were red,
and the frenzy of feeding that spring
will bring with the fingerling fry—
they will die in the dance of the riffle
or flee to the redds in the bed
       from mergansers, and herons, and gulls to endure
       as their myriads falter to fewer and fewer
       till they run for the sea and return when mature
to this bone-yard, from which they were bred.

Now is the time of the bones,
of your petrified gape. It bemoans
how the beaks picked your skeleton clean
as they pecked out your stomach and heart
through a grille-work of ventricle racks
on a spine that is chevroned with spines,
       leaving teeth that ripped herring-balls—blood, scale, and skin,
       leaving orbits your eyeballs were gimballed within
       and an arrowhead neb that was driven by fin
to be bonded by ice to these stones.

Now is the time of the bonds,
of the destinies twined like the fronds
in the lichen. Your whole generation,
who hailed from this valley, returned
and in thousands engaged in an orgy,
its climax a slough of despond's
       sh-sh-shudder as victims were swallowed—the strife
       as the spawning stress killed with its gralloching knife
       and you wallowed in currents that vied for your life,
with which time, the great river, absconds.

Catherine Tufariello

The Cricket in the Sump

He falls abruptly silent when we fling
A basket down or bang the dryer shut,
But soon takes up again where he left off.
Swept by a rainstorm through a narrow trough
Clotted with cobwebs into Lord knows what
Impenetrable murk, he's undeterred—
You'd think his dauntless solo was a chorus,
This rusty sump, a field or forest spring.
And there is something wondrous and absurd
About the way he does as he is bidden
By instinct, with his gift for staying hidden
While making sure unseen is plainly heard.

All afternoon his tremolo ascends
Clear to the second story, where a girl
Who also has learned blithely to ignore us
Sings to herself behind her bedroom door.
Maybe she moves to her invented score
With a conductor's flourish, or pretends
She's a Spanish dancer, lost in stamp and whirl
And waving fan—notes floating, as she plays,
Through the open window where the willow sways
And shimmers, humming to another string.
There is no story where the story ends.
What does a singer live for but to sing?

Kevin Corbett

Nature

The crush and draw of bone on rock,
The entrails poured out on the street
Emblazoned with the aftershock
Of blood that crusts in summer heat,
Not wholly red, not wholly blue—
This dead raccoon is Nature too.

The cherry tries to bloom in March,
The stinger tears out from the bee.
Hearing a sparrow leave its perch,
The rhino charges at a tree.
Beyond the beauty and the pith,
This is what we are dealing with.

She doesn't mean to drown the ants
Or leave the field-birds underfed,
Nor would she leave so much to chance,
Playing cat's cradle with the thread
Of life and death, were she aware
Her lethal nature is unfair.

Though even stoics like the shade
Of crisscross branches in a park,
They seek the roads that men have made
When Nature calls them toward the dark,
Waving an esoteric hand
Toward things no one can understand.

FICTION

Emily Cutler
Relativity

I skip graduation. In the Atlanta airport newsstand I try to find a *Cosmo Español* to read on the way over. I look through rows of women's fashion and beauty magazines: *Glamour, Self, Lucky, Vogue*. They're all in English, which makes them useless. I glance at the novels, the horrors by Steven King and the Harlequin romance novels by authors under pen names. *Return to Love. Scandal at the Balfour Ball.* My ninth grade history teacher writes Harlequin romance novels under a pseudonym. Sometimes, when I'm in the bookstore, I pick one up, read page 69, and try to guess if it could be by her.

My stepmother, Kelly, stands at the counter for different types of gum. She taps her foot as she scans the packages with her eyes. She turns over a green pack, reads the back of it. When she turns it back over she looks up and sees me. "Did you find anything?" she asks, pushing her short blonde hair behind her ears.

I shake my head. "No. It's all in English."

"You know, it's not a crime to read things in English."

"I'm not going to learn anything from a fashion magazine if it's in English."

Kelly picks up a magenta pack of gum, this time keeping it in her hand. "You don't have to learn something from everything you read. You know, you're supposed to read stupid, mindless stuff on planes. You don't have to make your mind work all the time."

I shrug. "I don't want to waste your money. It's not that long of a plane ride anyway."

She laughs. "This is about the longest plane ride you could take and still stay in the country."

"Yeah, I guess. I'll be fine." I look at my watch. "We should get over to the gate. Boarding starts in five minutes."

She buys the pack of gum and we jog up a flight of stairs until we arrive at the gate. The unaccompanied minors are already lined up at the front desk. The little girl at the front of the line rocks back and forth as if she needs to use the restroom. Technically, I should be doing the same, or at least feel as jittery internally. But I feel calm, as if I have just eaten a platter of sushi for dinner and am now going home to watch *Pride and Prejudice*. I guess it just hasn't hit me yet.

Over the speaker, the airport worker calls the A group to board the plane to Columbus. She has a Russian accent. Kelly faces me, her eyes concerned now. "Call me when you get there, okay?" I nod. "Good luck," she says.

She stands awkwardly, as if waiting for something. I just smile. Eventually she moves aside, and I line up in the A section. I used to hate Kelly. In my mind she was the reason that my parents had broken up. I didn't understand how she could sleep with my dad; I couldn't fathom why she had done something so shitty to my mom, to me. Sometimes I still want to tear her eyes out when I see her. But those times I have to backtrack, stop and think, realize that I, too, have loved a married man.

I inch forward in line and at last reach the front desk. The woman is hugely overweight and has short red frizzy hair. She rests her elbow on the desk, her hand under her chin. As she scans my boarding pass I twist around and shout "thank you!" to Kelly, but I don't think she hears me. I face forward again, and the woman gives me back my boarding pass. I walk ahead into the long, cold hallway. In my head I remember the product rule. *"F" times "G" prime plus "G" times "F" prime.*

★ ★ ★

I don't know what my mother despised more about my riding horses: that I had over a seventy percent chance of breaking my neck, or that I spent every afternoon and weekend at the barn with Gary. One day, on the way home from school, after a man had broken a picture frame in her coffee shop, so that she was already irritable, she told me that if Gary's wife ever met me, she would call me a slut. "She and I both know there's more to this than you're letting on, Elisa. And even if there isn't, just the appearance of impropriety is bad enough." I remember I wanted to punch through the windows of the car.

My mother never complained about the time I spent with Gary and the physical danger of horseback riding at the same time. While I was being fitted for my cast the first time I broke my leg, she just sat in a chair on the side of the room, drumming her fingers angrily on the arms. Every few minutes she would flip a page of *Southern Living* loudly, like a bolt of lightning. When the technician left the room she threw down the magazine and yelled at me for being selfish by making her watch me get hurt. "I want you to quit," she shouted. I was prepared for her to launch into a rant about Gary, but she didn't say a word about him.

My mother was nice to Gary to his face, like she was to everyone. When he walked me to her car late at night after my riding lesson, he would crouch down to look at her through the window, one hand resting in a fist on his ragged jeans, the other holding his leather hat upside down. He would say, "Elisa did good today. She's comin' along real well." My mother would smile and thank him like his compliment meant the world to her. Then she would drive off and rant about how he was married and unscrupulous, and uneducated and dirty, and how if it weren't for my dad I would never be allowed around such an asshole.

In middle school, both my parents supported my riding because it was the only time I wasn't angry. In high school, my mother became less supportive and thought I needed to find other ways to cope with my anger. My dad still supported my riding, however, and paid for the upkeep of my horse and my lessons. Some of the lessons were on the days my mother had custody, and she felt she had no choice but to take me.

★ ★ ★

I take a window seat in row seven. A few minutes later a tall guy in his early twenties sits in the seat next to me. His fingers are long and thin like his body. He wears thick black glasses and has a pen behind his ear. After taking his computer out of the case and setting it on his lap, he turns toward me.

"Hello, my name is Michael Westbrook." His voice is deep and thick. He sounds professional, as if he's interviewing me to be his business partner. When I was younger I always hoped people would do this on planes. I thought that everyone should want to meet everyone else.

"Uh, I'm Elisa," I say before realizing I probably shouldn't tell him my real name.

"Nice to meet you." He holds out his hand, and it takes me a minute to realize I'm supposed to shake it. "So, Elisa, what brings you to Ohio?"

I stare at him. He casually crosses his arms over his chest and looks at me expectantly. "Uh, well, I'm, uh, I'm going to see a friend. He works in Ohio. He does construction work."

"Construction work. That sounds interesting." He looks at me again, and I look away. Maybe I should try to pretend to fall asleep. "I'm sorry if this whole conversation seems random," he says. "I'm actually part of this project, and I have to meet three thousand people for an art exhibit. You're person number one. I'm not exactly sure how to go about this."

I face him again. "Next time, you could just come out and say that. And then start up the conversation."

He laughs and uncrosses his arms. "Yeah, maybe I should've done that."

"So why do you have to meet three thousand people for an art project?"

He picks up his laptop case again, pulls out a white index card, and hands it to me. I turn it over in my hands. On the back is a stamp and lines with an address in Philadelphia. "Write a piece of advice on it. Any advice that someone gave you or you just tend to live by. We're going to post three thousand of them on a display in Philadelphia. The spectators will each get to choose one to take home and keep."

I nod. "So what's the purpose of this?"

"I guess I just wanted to give three thousand random people a voice."

"You just woke up one morning and thought of that?"

"Kind of."

We laugh. The flight attendant's mechanical voice sounds over the loudspeaker. My mother once told me to apply the instructions they give you on the airplane to life. Don't help anyone else with their safety mask until you have your own on. The plane accelerates and takes off.

★ ★ ★

Gary taught me how to canter. Before I cared about my college application, in middle school, I spent every day all summer at the barn. My dad had custody in the summer, and he let me do whatever I wanted. One day, the summer after sixth grade, it was raining and Trevor was stomping because of the flies. I asked Gary if he thought it would be best for me not to ride. Normally he agreed with me in those situations, but that day he simply said, "Naw." I didn't question it. Instead I hopped on the saddle and rode around the ring. Gary took his usual position in the center of the ring with the whip.

After I had trotted for a while, he said, "I think it's 'bout time for you to learn to canter." I pulled back on the reins without even slowing to a walk. Rain fell heavily.

"You ain't supposed to stop, now. I told you you gotta start with a walk, but you can't just stop."

"I know *that*. It's just, why now? Weren't you going to, like, prepare me or something?"

He grinned, showing his crooked bottom teeth. "Well, you've been wantin' to canter for quite some time now, and I just decided that you're ready. You still want to, right?"

I nodded eagerly and began to walk. He cracked his whip against the ground one time. I thought that Trevor was bucking, that I was going to fall off. For the first time in years I reached for the horn and grabbed it. I squeezed my eyes shut, praying to God that I wouldn't fall. "That's it," Gary shouted. "Just hold on to the horn. Now move your body to the gait. One-two-three. Think three beats, like a waltz. Just like a waltz." Then I opened my eyes and realized that I was balanced.

After the lesson, we sat on the porch of the barn. He drank his usual beer; I drank my Diet Coke. I considered this an extremely normal ritual. The fact that he drank beer was just like the fact that he wore spurs on the back of his boots. I never told my parents or my friends just because I didn't think it was a big deal.

The flies buzzed loudly, and I repeatedly inhaled dust. "I can't believe I really did it," I said after I had taken my first sip.

"You did," he said, leaning back in his white chair. "You should be proud, cowgirl. Tell them bullies at school they don't matter 'cause you can canter."

"Was I really cantering? Did it really look like I was cantering?"

"Sure it did. You did pretty good for your first time." I smiled. I felt like nothing else mattered. Earlier I had been scared to go back to school in two weeks, but I wasn't anymore. I was Elisa Kates, and I could canter, and I was good at it. It didn't matter what anyone else thought.

Fluency must be like cantering. I imagine that once you reach it, you're invincible.

★ ★ ★

Next to me, Michael types on his laptop. He types at a steady rhythm with only two fingers. "So why are you visiting your friend in Ohio?"

"Uh, I don't know, really. I just really wanted to see him."

He nods, lacing his fingers together, as if he's analyzing me. "Did he used to live in Marietta?"

"Yeah."

"Went to school with you?"

I shake my head. "He was my horseback riding instructor."

"Oh. So you guys have been keeping in touch ever since he moved?"

I nod at first.

"That's so cool that you have that kind of relationship," he says.

I crack my fingers. "Yeah. I mean, we haven't gotten to keep in touch that much. I used to write him letters."

"Oh." He pauses, stretching his arms so that the backs of his hands interlace sideways. "I'm sure you're both really busy."

"Yeah. He has so much to do, I bet. He went to Ohio to do construction work. He's probably on top of ladders all the time. And he has his wife with him, and so I'm sure he's spending a lot of time with her, and for all I know they could have...." I stop myself. He would have written me for something big like that. Michael gives me a quick nod, smiling nervously, before he resumes typing. After a long silence, I say, "He's a good man."

"You know this?"

"It's an absolute truth."

★ ★ ★

Months before he left, I decided for my junior year community service project I wanted to be a volunteer barn hand for Gary. I would leave two days a week at lunch for the barn to have a total of twenty-four hours of community service my junior year. He loved the idea at first.

In the nights before I brought him the official papers, I dreamt the most intense scenarios. One night I dreamt we were having our usual post-lesson drink when a fly landed on my cheek and wouldn't budge. Gary lifted his hand and brushed it along my cheek, flicking it away gently. When it was gone, he didn't remove his hand. Another night I had to climb a ladder in the tack room for more saddle soap. He held my hand as he helped me up the ladder, but when I came back down, he kept holding it. I would wake up sweating.

I gave him the papers on Thursday. He sat on the porch, having just finished teaching another lesson. Although he was only in his early thirties, sometimes, after lessons, he looked older. His straw hat covered his scruffy brown hair, and his blue eyes drooped downward. Dirt rested in the creases of his hands and under his fingernails.

"Basically you just have to sign that this is a volunteer service and you're not paying me," I started. He took off his hat, and I knew something was wrong. I knew what was wrong before he said it.

"You know what people have been saying about me and you. Parents at the barn, the other guys. I gotta be careful, Elisa. You're not a little girl no more, and I gotta—I just have to be careful. I can't spend so much time with you like I used to. You—you grew up, and things are all different now."

I couldn't breathe.

"You understand, right?" he asked, after he finished explaining.

I nodded, digging my nails into my arm to try not to cry. I counted my mistakes. If I hadn't stayed up so late talking to him on the phone last month. If I hadn't gone on the trail ride alone with him last week. If I hadn't smiled so broadly when I came to the barn with the papers. I pushed my teeth together, like chewing sand.

"Life ain't fair, Elisa. If I was a girl and you were a guy, it would all be different. No one would say nothing."

"Should I come to the barn less?" I asked.

"Naw. 'Course not. You're still my only student who owns her own horse, so you got more of a right to be 'round here than anyone else."

"Even though I'm the only girl at your barn."

"Even though."

I couldn't do any homework that night. I cried into my pillow. I broke a pencil, but that didn't even go near releasing any of my anger. After that Gary made excuses to skip our post-lesson drink.

He moved away a few months later. Sometimes I can't stop speculating on why. Did his wife demand it? Were there too many complaints from the other riders? I can't help thinking it was because of me, which makes me want to stop talking again.

★★★

Chances are my dad will be late to graduation. This means that when he arrives he will think my name has already been called. This also means that my mother will be too angry with his tardiness to notice my absence during the ceremony. After the ceremony, when my mother has verbally attacked my dad for a sufficient amount of time, they will start to look for me. Kelly will tell them I had plans for lunch with my friends and have already left.

My mother will wear her typical dressy skirt. It is the skirt she bought at the thrift store when we took a trip to Iowa City for her college reunion. I was only seven. Still she wears that skirt to every graduation, wedding, and funeral that she is invited to. My mother will brush the knots out of her matted brown hair and wear it down instead of a bun like she does for work. She will wear heels and she will wear mascara and blush. I picture her sitting in a purple chair in the auditorium with a program in her lap, nodding approvingly at the listing of "Harvard" next to my name.

My dad will wake up and forget it is the day of my graduation. He will dress in his clothes for the office, a casual shirt and khakis. Just as he is about to leave, he will see the invitation to my graduation still on the refrigerator, and he will sprint back to his room to change. I picture him, scrambling for a tie, accidentally picking the yellow one and frantically tying it around his neck.

I look at my watch. Graduation starts in fifteen minutes. I picture Kelly speeding down the highway, her windows down and Kanye West booming over the radio. In my head I repeat the quadratic formula. *Negative "b" plus or minus the square root of "b" squared minus four "a" "c" over two "a."*

★★★

When Dr. Evans told me if I had fallen in even a slightly different position I would have died, I laughed. My mother stood up and kicked her chair. Dr. Evans ran his fingers through his gray hair and yawned. He said, "You know the procedure by now. I'll send a tech in to fit you to a neck brace. I'll give you a heavier dose of painkillers this time. It's going to feel a lot worse since it's your neck. You should be able to get back to riding in six to eight months." My mother left the room and slammed the door.

By then it was my senior year, and I had already applied to Harvard. I was riding English with a new instructor, and I could jump almost as well as I could rope. But it all felt so new still.

Gary didn't answer my calls. I had stopped writing him about a month ago, but I decided to try one last time. I would make my appeal with humor. A week after I broke my neck, I wrote, "You were right about riding English. Here you thought it was bad that I broke my leg every time I fell riding Western. I was just jumping, and guess what? I broke my neck. Dr. Evans said I almost died. Do you remember him?" Maybe I had the wrong address.

I sold my horse to a five-year-old boy in Nashville, Tennessee. I told my friends the doctor said I couldn't ever ride again. Kelly said not to worry, that in a few years, after college, if I was ready to ride again, it would be easy to go back. "You won't always be scared," she would say. I wanted to tear her eyelashes off her eyelids when she said that. When I got my acceptance letter from Harvard, my mother said that quitting horseback riding paid off. "You were able to put so much more dedication into your schoolwork. It was such a smart move. I told you all along."

My friends said, "It's so good that you're like the perfect student. I mean, it's really sad that you can't horseback ride anymore, but at least you still have something."

★ ★ ★

The seatbelt sign turns off with a ding. Michael pulls down his tray and puts his laptop on it. I stare at the white rectangle in front of me, trying to think of what advice I should give to a stranger.

My mother would say, "Always put yourself first. Your health, your safety, your education. Don't make decisions because you think it would benefit someone else."

My dad would say, "Put happiness first. That's what's most important in life."

Kelly would say, "Don't worry so much. Just go do your shit and have a damn fun time while you're doing it."

Gary would say, "Stay in the now—not the last now, not the next now; this now."

★ ★ ★

After my mother sent in the deposit to Harvard, Kelly took me out to Outback Steakhouse and bought me a beer. It tasted sour, but I drank the whole thing anyway. When I finished, I asked, "Why the hell did I decide to go to Harvard next year?"

Kelly laughed. "Because you're a dumbass."

★ ★ ★

"So where all are you traveling?" I ask Michael.

"I start out with Ohio. Then I'm driving to Kentucky, and from there I'm just making my way down South."

"How long will you stay in each state?"

"Two days. After that I'm going to the East Coast, so I'll get to go through places like Connecticut and D.C."

"That's a long time away from home."

"I have to meet a lot of people. And besides, I've always wanted to travel around the country before I die."

"People only say that when they're old."

"I feel old."

I catch a glimpse of the screen of his laptop. "Spark Notes?" I ask jokingly.

"Yeah, that's another one of those do-before-you-die things of mine. Not Spark Notes. Books. I want to read all the classics, or at least what people think of as the classics. For now I'm just reading the Spark Notes."

"Doesn't that ruin it?"

He looks at his laptop. "You know, I originally wanted people to write their secrets on the postcard. But then the Post Secret website stole my idea."

"Secret is just a romanticized way to say lie."

He laughs. "I've never thought about it that way before."

"I'll tell you my secret if you'll tell me yours."

He looks up from his laptop, eyes squinted and forehead creased, as if I had just tried to tell him we are actually on the ground, not in the air. But then he kind of smiles. "You go first."

"I'm skipping graduation right now."

"Really? Your high school graduation?"

"Yeah. It's your turn."

"I have six months to live."

★ ★ ★

Sometimes, on Saturday mornings, I wake up and dress in my jeans and old riding boots, and I get in the car and drive the familiar route to the barn. I drive past the mall, past the Dairy Queen, past the gas station connected with the Subway. Then I'm in the country, where every minute I see a farm with horses. I admire them, try to guess what type and how old they are. I pull up at my barn, and it's only when I don't see Gary's pickup truck that I realize it's the present. Then I turn around in my car and hope no one saw me.

★ ★ ★

"Am I the first person you told about that?"

"So what if you are?"

"Then I'm person number one twice. I kind of feel special."

★ ★ ★

I was a problem child in fifth grade. It was the year my parents split up, and the year I stopped talking when I wasn't answering someone.

My mother brought me to a psychologist who wore glasses on her neck and had games like Parcheesi and Trouble stacked in her office. She had a high-pitched voice when she talked to me and a somewhat deeper voice when she talked to my parents. I hated her. I hated that she took my parents into her office for private conversations specifically about me, and I hated that she told me, in a mechanical voice, it wasn't possible for my parents to get back together.

My dad took me out for ice cream at Dairy Queen on the weekends. I thought ice cream was annoying so I always ordered a small box of French Fries. My dad brought Kelly once but I didn't talk the entire time so he never brought her again. He tried to convince me that divorce could be fun. I would get two houses, and I would never get bored of living at one place because I could just go to the other. It would almost be like having two moms, too. When he said this I shut up for the rest of the night.

My friends didn't really understand what was going on. I think they just thought I was angry all the time. I was. That was the year I began being angry.

I wasn't angry when I was at the barn, though. In the summer, when I didn't say a word during an entire two-hour lesson, Gary made me dismount and he talked to me for a long time on the porch. "It ain't your fault, Elisa," he said. And although I was accustomed to discarding that statement, on that particular day I tried to believe it.

★ ★ ★

The flight attendant stops in the aisle next to our row. "Would you like a beverage?" she asks. For an inexplicable reason the word "libation" pops into my head, and I remember when we learned the word as part of our vocabulary lesson in sixth grade. It was the day after my dad's birthday, and he let me have a sip of his champagne at dinner. I told a friend that "I had an alcoholic libation last night." My English teacher overheard me and sent me to the principal's office.

I stifle a laugh. "I'll have a Diet Coke." Michael orders water.

★ ★ ★

The summer before my junior year, after Gary left, I made a list of questions to ask him. Why will horses suddenly stop before they jump when they do fine with barrels? Why does the long trot feel so much more natural than the posting trot? Am I supposed to actually like showing? Is there any way to get Trevor to canter more slowly? Are Stubben saddles really better than other types of saddles, or just a bigger name? Have you ever been forced to wear English riding pants, and were they this uncomfortable for you? Why do

English riders get so angry when you say "whoa" when you're trying to get a horse to stop? What should I say to people who call me stupid because of my four on the chemistry AP exam? Should I tour Harvard over Fall Break? Can't a young girl fall in love with someone older? Should I go on a college road trip with Kelly, even if I still haven't forgiven her?

★ ★ ★

I gaze out the window. The Earth looks like a life-sized map, and it's hard to force myself to believe I am only looking at one area of one state, not the whole world. I trace my fingers around the circular, almost flower-shaped lakes. I run my fingers along the rivers, curving only slightly. I carve squares around the patches of grass, around the skyscraper buildings.

I watch the cars. I can only see the tops, the shiny red, black, silver, and green of each. I could take one in my palm and lift it up at any moment. In one area, shiny dots of red, black, silver, green, and white cover a dull black surface. It takes me a minute to realize it's a parking lot.

The houses are miniature. It must be impossible to see a person, but I silently pray to see one anyway. I look at the houses, and when I glance back at a road, a girl walks her dog. I can't see her face, or even what clothes she wears. She looks like a doll that I have dropped off a balcony. This is what it must be like to be a giant.

And then, out of nowhere, it hits me that to that girl, this plane is the size of a bird, and I fit inside it.

"Oh," I say accidentally.

"What?" says Michael.

In AP European History we learned that Einstein's Theory of Relativity meant that life went at different speeds depending whether you were inside a train or out of it. Something like that. I didn't understand the specifics; I just memorized the exact textbook wording for the test.

Now, if I measured the road from here, it might be a few inches. If a person on the ground measured, it would probably be miles. Neither measurement would be accurate.

When we land, I will walk through the hallway to the airport. I will pick up my suitcase at the baggage claim, and then I will roll it up the stairs of the shuttle. When I arrive at the inn, I will turn on my phone and call Kelly.

BOOK REVIEW

Julie Stoner

Maxine Kumin, *Where I Live:*
New & Selected Poems 1990-2010
W.W. Norton, 2010
ISBN 978-0-393-07649-3, USA $29.95

Carrie Jerrell, *After the Revival*
Waywiser, 2009
ISBN 978-1-904130-38-3, USA $15.00

★ ★ ★

After the Revival, Carrie Jerrell's 2008 Anthony Hecht Award-winning book, reminds me of an after-school snack I used to scarf down in the 1980s, as the kitchen radio provided a soundtrack of honky-tonk and static. First, nuke about ¼ cup canned or leftover chili. Open an individual-sized bag of Fritos brand corn chips and spoon the chili directly into it. Top with a vinyl square of American cheese and a splash of hot sauce. Eat with a spoon, right out of the crinkly bag.

This lowbrow delicacy is not to everyone's taste, and I daresay neither is *After the Revival*. Personally, I enjoyed the combination of salt and crunch and grease and hellfire and cheese, even if I had to overcome the occasional wave of nausea. (I'm still referring to the book.)

To continue the food metaphor, I would characterize Maxine Kumin's *Where I Live: New & Selected Poems 1990-2010* as a rustic New England bean soup at base, jazzed up with occasional exotic surprises like chorizo and cilantro and . . . I pause to consider some particularly fiery pieces about animal abuse and human torture . . . perhaps a splash of too much Tabasco.

Both poets do interesting things with rhyme and meter and form, and have deservedly found enthusiastic fans. But not everyone will find these books palatable, either in terms of ingredients or execution.

★★★

This seems a convenient time to revisit the running argument I have with an otherwise astute and agreeable friend. He holds that it is inappropriate for reviewers to say whether or not they "liked" a particular film or book. Not only does my killjoy friend condemn *pleasure* as a hopelessly subjective criterion, he deems it irrelevant where art is concerned. Sophisticated critics understand that the role of the artist is to challenge audiences, not necessarily to *please* them. Many important works of art were never intended to be likeable, so to state that one liked or disliked a particular artistic endeavor is, in my friend's view, to announce that one has missed the point. He further opines that, when evaluating the artistic merit of a piece, one must take care not to be distracted by one's affinity—or lack thereof—for its subject matter. A truly gifted artist can take even the most repugnant material and make a masterpiece of it. Style transcends substance.

I counter that one's personal response to the subject matter . . . matters. However inspired the omelet, individual diners have the right to intensely dislike eggs. And if eggs dominate the menu at a trendy new restaurant, should a conscientious reviewer refrain from mentioning that fact? Ridiculous.

I also contend that the role of the reviewer is not to promote art and culture to people too ignorant to know what's good for them, but to help potential audience members make informed decisions about how to spend their limited time and money. True, erudite critics have often helped me to appreciate an aspect of a work that would otherwise be lost on me, so I acknowledge reviewers' didactic function. But assessing the likelihood of my deriving *pleasure* from a film or book remains my main objective when I read reviews.

As you may have noticed, this attitude also taints my writing of them.

★★★

Ahem. So, if you are like my resolutely unbiased friend, you will not blink at the preponderance of poems on gardening and animal husbandry in Maxine Kumin's 229-page *Where I Live: New and Selected Poems 1990-2010*—an assemblage of her greatest hits from the collections *Looking for Luck (1992)*, *Connecting the Dots (1996)*, *The Long Marriage (2003)*, *Jack and Other New Poems (2003)*, and *Still to Mow (2007)*, plus 23 new poems. You will cast a dispassionate eye on the graphic veterinary treatise that begins "The Taste of Apple":

> After the year of come-and-go nosebleeds, after
> daily washing mucousy blood from his forelegs and flanks
> where he swiped himself clean in his impatient horsey way,
> I saw the tumor sprout waxy and white
> out of one nostril and dangle there, a rare fruit.
> Truth rose in my mouth, a drench of gall and wormwood
> and I sent for the vet and the backhoe driver
> who came together like football coaches conferring.

With equally admirable detachment, you will consider the Cushing's-afflicted old broodmare *squatting, crooking and lifting her tail,/ squirting urine and winking her vulva, all// classic signs of estrus* in "The Winking Vulva." And, having dutifully traversed poems like "Hay" and "Chores" and "Mulching" before reaching "The Zen of Mucking Out" on page 195, you will lack the temerity to think that this is the (dirty) straw that finally pushes the homespun narrator's *smeary load* right on over the top.

Of course you wouldn't entertain such an unworthy thought. Shame on me for even suggesting it. But I spent my childhood slaving away on my parents' small ranch, and my own less-than-ecstatic experience of farmyard drudgery has left my objectivity sadly compromised.

To be fair, Kumin delves into plenty of other subjects in addition to her workaday life in rural New Hampshire. (Having already devoted a 206-page prose memoir, *Inside the Halo and Beyond: The Anatomy of a Recovery*, to the 1998 horse-carriage accident in which she broke her neck, Kumin makes only two or three oblique references to it in this collection spanning 1990-2010.) When not obsessing about her horses, dogs, and garden, Kumin considers her Jewish religious and cultural heritage, particularly in contrast with her education at the Catholic school next door to her childhood home in Philadelphia. She explores current and past family relationships, along with some rather steamy encounters from her youth. She looks back on her eighteen-year friendship and collaboration with poet Anne Sexton, along with her thirty-six-year struggle to come to terms with Sexton's suicide. And she reflects on other poetic influences as well: five poems are devoted to Wordsworth and/or Coleridge, and individual poems reference Longfellow ("The Victorian Obsession with the Preservation of Hair"), W. H. Auden ("The Symposium"), Hopkins ("Almost Spring, Driving Home, Reciting Hopkins"), and a generous handful of other literary luminaries. From her perspective as a former Consultant in Poetry to the Library of Congress (Kumin's tenure was 1981-1982, shortly before the position's name was changed to Poet Laureate), she considers the political fortunes of poets in China, Bulgaria, and elsewhere in our troubled world.

Where I Live contains a fair number of politically-charged pieces, some so scathing that they inspired my earlier reference to Tabasco sauce. The new poem "Waterboarding, Restored" is probably the tamest of the lot. It calmly discusses Kumin's decision to self-censor a poem on that subject, the initial stanza of which she quotes in its entirety. But the narrator acted on the advice of her editor: *Let's take this one out* [. . .] *two years from now/ (it takes that long to go from manuscript/ to print) no one will even remember/ the word.* "Waterboarding, Restored" suggests that Kumin's editor may have been partially right, but not, unfortunately, due to the torture method's obsolescence: *Now under the shellac/ of euphemism they're calling it/ enhanced interrogation* [. . .] *Only the mockingbird is cleverer/ warbling blithe lies from his tree.*

At the other end of the capsaicin heat spectrum, "Please Pay Attention as the Ethics Have Changed" interprets the Humane Society's statistics for Vice President Cheney's and Supreme Court Justice Scalia's infamous pheasant and duck expeditions: *this is canned hunting// where you don't stay to pluck/ the feathers, pull the innards out. Fuck// all of that. You don't do shit/ except shoot.* The narrator goes on to ask,

> But where is that other Humane Society, the one with rules
> we used to read aloud in school
>
> the one that takes away your license to collar
> and leash a naked prisoner
>
> the one that forbids you to sodomize
> a detainee before the cold eyes
>
> of your fellow MPs? [. . .]

The poem concludes, *The ethics have changed.// Fuck the Geneva Convention.* Perhaps not the typical musings of an 85-year-old New Hampshire farmwife.

But not entirely unexpected from the vegetarian mother of a United Nations translator. Cruelty to animals also segues directly into political violence in the poems "The Whole Hog" and "Game." And while "The Kentucky Derby," "Bringing Down the Birds," and the kitten- and puppy-discarding "Which One" focus on cruelty to animals, they do so in close proximity to, respectively, "Waterboarding, Restored," "Identifying the Disappeared," and "The Jew Order" (referencing General Grant's 1862 expulsion of Jews from Union Territory *for violating every regulation of trade*). The latter two pairings occupy facing pages.

For purists like my aforementioned friend, concerned primarily with style, I'll comment on Kumin's characteristic plainspokenness. Her heavily-enjambed, often-unmetrical approach can be starkly effective; however, when transferred to political and humanitarian topics, Kumin's lineated but otherwise prosaic outrage comes across as just plain preachy.

I much prefer the less strident voice of "Across the Estuary," a sleepy little poem in which the narrator lazily half-listens to the noise of a distant house under construction, before casually observing that the hammer's *satisfying thwacks* and the *singing* circular saw, *far away enough to soothe*, might have disturbing connotations: *I doze in the sun, confident/ no one is being nailed to a cross// today or having his arms/ chopped off above the elbows.*

You must have already read page 78 of *Inside the Halo* to link the latter reference to atrocities in Sierra Leone's civil war, because for some reason this tidbit is not noted in *Where I Live*. Perhaps Kumin's endnotes are so slender because she occasionally discusses individual poems in her five books of essays. Still, it would be nice to have more of this helpful background material . . . um . . . collected . . . in this collection, and in collections in general.

Why do so many poets and editors seem to feel that would be patronizing to provide readers with just a little more context? I'll revisit this issue when I discuss Jerrell's book.

★ ★ ★

But first, my friend would want to hear more about Kumin's style and technique. My own current stylistic obsession is with repetitive forms, and Kumin has generously provided several examples in *Where I Live*.

The self-contained, endstopped thoughts of "What You Do" are a better fit for the pantoum framework than the more conversational and enjambed "Pantoum, with Swan," which repeats only keywords in duplicate lines of varying length. Both poems demonstrate the form's characteristic surrealism, but I happen to prefer the one that takes fewer liberties with the form.

Similarly, Kumin's 1998 "Ghazal: On the Table"—a Persian form in which the final word or words of the second line of each couplet is repeated, preceded by a repeating rhyme—seems to have influenced Kumin's minimalist treatment of villanelles, and not always for the better. "The Domestic Arrangement," a 2006 villanelle bearing the subtitle *from Dorothy Wordsworth's journals*, emulates its prose source by dispensing with rhyme entirely and repeating only snatches of each repetend line. The new poem "Symposium" is another meanderingly meterless, rhymeless villanelle with keyword repetends. The form's repetitiveness successfully conjures the image of several experts trotting out the same old platitudes and anecdotes about W. H. Auden, so I suppose it still works as a villanelle.

Perhaps I'm too conservative, but these examples make me wonder: at what point does a poet decide that there is no longer enough meat left on the picked-over carcass of a form to justify serving it up as such? After consulting Kumin's variation-praising essay "Gymnastics: The Villanelle" in *Always Beginning*—an essay also available online via the Google Books version of *An Exaltation of Forms: Contemporary Poets Celebrate the Diversity of Their Art*, if you care to consult it, too—I remain undecided.

Despite my misgivings, Kumin disrupts the traditional rhyme scheme (A^1bA^2 abA^1 abA^2 abA^1 abA^2 abA^1A^2) far more purposefully and effectively in "Entering Houses at Night," a villanelle inspired by a young female Iraqi's blog dated February 11, 2006 (thank you, endnotes!), but actually told from the aggressors' point of view. The arbitrariness of a sweep for suspected insurgents is communicated through the replacement of the first two lines of each tercet with rhymed or unrhymed couplets. One of the poem's two repetends—*We went in punching kicking yelling out orders*—does not appear in the initial stanza at all, only bursting into the poem partway through to supplant *None of us spoke their language*, as if the two clauses were exact equivalents. I suppose they are, when the context is expanded beyond line-ends: *None of us spoke their language and/ none of them spoke ours* gives way to *We went in punching kicking yelling out orders// in our language, not theirs*. It is fitting that line-boundaries are not respected in the poem, given the other repetend: *We went in breaking down doors*.

Inconveniently for my thesis, Kumin's tinkering with the villanelle form long predates her 1998 ghazal. The first half of a double villanelle, "The Nuns of Childhood: Two Views" from 1992's *Looking for Luck*, commemorates *one harridan nun,/ fiercest of all the parochial coven, Sister Pascala*, who *had to be bodily restrained* from dispensing discipline *at random*. Kumin's alarmingly unrestrained repetends do not rhyme with each other, nor with the *a* lines of later stanzas, and only their last word or phrase repeats. The poem begins:

> O where are they now, your harridan nuns
> who thumped on young heads with a metal thimble
> and punished with rulers your upturned palms:
>
> three smacks for failing in long division,
> one more to instill the meaning of *humble*.
> As the twig is bent, said your harridan nuns.

Kumin's *b* rhymes incline toward stricter perfection over the course of the first villanelle—*thimble, humble, shambled, scramble, preamble, brambles*—but fall away from that perfection over the course of the second—*wimples, example, vestals, lolled, child*, and *gold*. Conversely, this marked relaxation correlates with a tightening of the repetends in the more positive second villanelle: *my darling nuns* rhyme where *your harridan nuns* had not (*inside their gowns*), even as Kumin further starches the tercets' outer garments by rhyming most of the *a* lines.

Experimentation with rhyme also enlivens Kumin's sestina about her young grandson's desire to change his own name. *Noah* seems to remain *Noah* only by virtue of not being an endword in his own poem: the name of his first-grade classmate, *Xuan Loc,* transmutes into *clock*, *block*, *lock*-[/ stepped], *lack*, and *unlock* before returning to *Xuan Loc*. Similarly, the uncertainty of *we can only guess* becomes more uncertain in its repetitions as *quest*, *guessed*, *Holy Ghost*, *guest*, *gassed*, and *quest*. Although Kumin has long used off-rhyme in poems featuring her trademarked couplets, I find it especially powerful in the sestina, where rhyme is not expected at all.

★ ★ ★

Sestina variations seem an ideal point of departure for changing horses (or poets) midstream, since Carrie Jerrell also tweaks the form in a unique way in *After the Revival*. "The Country-Western Singer's Ex-Wife, Sober in Mendocino County, California" replaces one of the six repeated endwords with a Willy Nelson song reference. Since she hums a different tune in each iteration, and since her book provides no endnotes whatsoever, I couldn't quite fathom what Jerrell was up to until I stumbled across her discussion of this poem at *From the Fishhouse: An Audio Archive of Emerging Poets* (http://www.fishousepoems.org/archives/carrie_jerrell/index.shtml).

Attention, poets and editors! Some of your customers resent being forced to conduct online searches for information that could easily have been provided in the books we've paid for. Why are you so maddeningly reluctant to provide us with contextual and stylistic notes? The hypothetical know-it-alls who might feel insulted by such aids could simply skip them, couldn't they? Surely you can afford to print an extra page or two, thereby adding much value to your product at minuscule cost. But I digress.

Even before I was able to crack Jerrell's code, I enjoyed the dynamism of her sestina's other end words—especially the much-traveled *boot*, with its hint that the singer's current lady friend will follow in the narrator's footsteps. The celebrity's ex-wife understands her rival's infatuation: *I've played her part, the starstruck blonde in boots// and denim mini, boobs and brains to boot*, but the narrator also remembers the rejection that followed. Reflecting on her isolation after the singer dumped her and *left me listening to "Sad Songs and Waltzes," Waylon, steel guitars that struck like a boot/ to the face*, the narrator revisits her anger: *I'd be lying/ if I said I didn't want to fill my ex's boots/ with spit the night I caught him with that up-/ start starlet at the bar*. But rage gives way to depression as *all the songs I loved—"Crazy,"/ "Golden Ring," "Jolene"—became like boots/ too busted to put on*. Although the narrator claims to have moved on—*I've burned my boots*—she admits that *I still wake up/ to his tunes: the beer, blow, boots and love*. The sestina's recursive nature reinforces the notion that other women will be doomed to repeat the narrator's frustrating history with this man, and that the narrator herself can't quite break free, either.

Although not in a repeating form, "What Goes Around" also explores the cyclical nature of romantic breakups. The poem begins with literal circling: *You're leaving a city you never could call home,/ cruising the concrete noose of its Outer Loop,/ marveling that everything you own fits in your pick-up,/ when you notice you're four exits past your exit.* Deeming it easier to continue driving the crowded six-lane loop than to fight her way over to an off-ramp and turn back, the protagonist has ample time to observe the argument of a couple in a neighboring car. *You can tell/ by the way he jabs his finger in her face/ and she smacks the dash with the flats of her hands/ that they aren't singing with the music.* By virtue of the second-person narration, each reader has already been baptized as an alter ego, but now the arguing woman in the next lane becomes one as well: *Caught looking, you catch a glimpse of something/ you saw in yourself just last year.* This literal and figurative fellow-traveler reminds the narrator of not one, but three, instances of her own spiteful behavior during breakups—my favorite of which is *further back, in college,/ when you pulled a Delilah on your three-chord,/ "rock star" boyfriend, leaving his locks to curl/ like vipers on your vacated pillow.* At this point, one might begin to wonder why the narrator's pick-up truck just happens to be loaded with everything she owns, and why she was so distracted as to miss her exit in the first place, but the poem does not volunteer additional information. The second stanza (of four) compares the circularity of retribution to the circularity of addiction: *Revenge. <u>The big black pill</u>, your grandfather called it/ from the pulpit, <u>and God alone should give out/ the prescription.</u>* But the narrator, *Being born an addict*, knows that *Love's a dealer, too.*

The scenario in "Big Daddy" is similar to that of the sestina: a woman deals with a musician's dumping of her. However, this narrator exorcises her missing mate more aggressively:

> Small likenesses of you croak to me
>
> from their lilypadded thrones. I'd like to mistake
> their bellows for green apologies, but I know better.
>
> At night, I hunt them with a three prong. I fry them
> in batter and grease. We both know what they taste like.

Yet another woman unlucky in love grinds the gears of "Demolition Derby" out of its loose iambic pentameter and into occasional tet or hex lines, recklessly pairing such rhyme words as *minutes/spinouts* and *shitless/broadside hits*. The rhymes become more perfect as the narrator, initially characterized as *the candy stuck in a steel piñata, shitless/ scared but falling for the spinouts*, leaves *that first race, that boy* in the past. However, this young thrill-seeker won't give up her adrenaline addiction, and *the busted lip* seems ominous evidence that she has yet to find a winning partnership in either love or racing.

★★★

Long titles and disturbing topics abound in Jerrell's 44-poem collection. *But my home county's overrun/ with tweakers cooking bathtub crank in houses/ one dropped cigarette away from bursting/ into flame,* we hear in "For the Sparrows Who Lost Their Nests in the Southern Indiana Tornado." "The Poet Prays to the 9mm under the Driver's Seat" is a chilling paean to the handgun that will stop the suicidal narrator's heart: *Coldest friend, pretty little monster,/ I know relief lies low and left of center. [. . .] You have a way with wounds,// with damage and deliverance, and I make/ a ready berm for both.* The prize for the longest title goes to the Petrarchan sonnet "Bill Moore Removes Leeches from My Legs after I Ignore His Advice and Walk My Kayak Ashore through Leaf Cover"—also a contender in the disturbing topic category. But that trophy belongs to "In an Indiana County Thick with Copperheads," for the lines *Tweaked out on her mother's meth,/ the twelve-year-old walks/ the county roads of my childhood,/ [. . .] the teeth/ of the mottled Lab less frightening than/ her uncle and his bristle-brush whiskers.*

Perhaps my pedantic friend is right, and I shouldn't allow myself to be distracted by the subject matter of *After the Revival*. It shouldn't matter that Jerrell's birth year (1976) is also that of my horse-crazy little sister, and that Jerrell's characters mirror the bizarre mix of alcoholic and evangelical trailer trash with whom my siblings and I came of age in our microscopic town in the Mojave Desert. But, considering the desperation with which we four Stoner girls sought scholarships in order to escape a version of the milieu Jerrell captures so bleakly, my response can't help but be subjective. The typical reader will probably not be so personally affected by descriptions like *The trailer I grew up in sits alone, abandoned/ at the edge of town like a whiskered old man/ watching lightning from a busted lawn chair* ("For the Sparrows . . ."). Curiously, my thesaurus lists no antonyms for "nostalgia". Will "the screaming heebie-jeebies" do?

But surely one does not need to share my background to share my distaste for the sheer over-the-topitude of "The Poet Prays to Her Radio for a Country Song":

> Traveling the long tongue of highway 40,
> I fear the bottomless black sky of loneliness
> has hawked me from the back of its throat
> and doomed me to land, wet and without notice,
> in the dust-bitten spittoon of Oklahoma.

Although I admire many of Jerrell's turns of phrase in the same poem—*once again I've let heartbreak/ put his hands in my back pockets*, for example, or *Let my voice be open/ as a screen door, all latchless and breeze-blown,/ all invitation*—I find the extended throat-clearing metaphor just a tad too much.

My favorite part of *After the Revival* is the dark humor of Jerrell's twenty-sonnet series on weddings. The cleverly circular composition of "The Father of the Bride" begins *When the tailor's club hand hovers near the crotch/ of a penguin suit worth more than your last Winchester* and ends with *another budget-busting coup* by the bride, *your little girl, who's always had you by the balls*. In "The Ring," Jerrell notes that wedding bands, *once standard 14k gold, now come/ in weapons-grade titanium*. And here's a memorable scene from "The Bouquet Toss": *when all/ the girls press in as close as they can get,/ you think of tip-offs, high school basketball,/ your mother's scream, <u>Get on the floor for it!</u>* Depressingly soon, this hopeful scrimmage turns into *another/ pathetic loss to some sixteen-year-old,/ fresh, thin, and better built to play this game*. But defeat is inevitable, anyway, as we see in the final couplet of "The Recessional": *the groom carries his bride so her train won't drag./ The wind unfurls it like a big white flag*.

★ ★ ★

Though it may seem too little, too late, to placate my fair-minded friend, I'll conclude this discussion of *Where I Live* and *After the Revival* by keeping my subjectivity to myself, for once. I'll simply juxtapose the endings of two poems.

Here are the final lines of Kumin's "Perspective," a 22-line ekphrasis of George Stubb's monumental portrait of Whistlejacket (http://www.nationalgallery.org.uk/paintings/george-stubbs-whistlejacket), a dun racehorse who stands on nothing as he rears against a neutral background:

> O horse of my heart, hang on at this still point
> as all around us open-air markets explode,
>
> body parts rain down and families
> rush to collect them, else no afterlife.
>
> The priest insists that animals are sinless,
> have no souls, won't appear in heaven,
>
> *his* heaven, not the paradise
> of expectant virgins. Where
>
> Whistlejacket went is
> not revealed, into the ground,
>
> perhaps, in his final pasture,
> O horse of my heart, full nine feet tall.

And here are the final lines of Jerrell's "I Am Thinking of My First Horse," also 22 lines long, which begins *A dun, his body the only kingdom/ I know the whole of*:

> because I imagine he waits on the bank
> to carry me, I am thinking of my first horse,
> how we will leave our scars in the water
> behind us, entering a kingdom we praise
> but cannot ever fully know.
> I am thinking of my first horse
> because I want no heaven without him.

BOOK REVIEW

John Whitworth

Jeff Chaucer, *A Garden of Erses: Limericks*
Introduced by Robert Conquest

Orchises (Washington)

$12.95

A Book of Erses by Jeff Chaucer is ... what? It doesn't take a great deal of nous to spot that Jeff Chaucer if a pseudonym, though I have to confess I have no idea what Erses are. On the back of the book is a short encomium by Philip Larkin and on the inside pages the author thanks, among others, Kingsley Amis and Philip Larkin, and also Robert Conquest, Victor Gray and Ted Pauker. All this puzzled the reviewer in *The Spectator* who complained the limericks were not attributed, so he had no idea who had written which.

Well now, let me see. Victor Gray, anagrammatized, gives us G.R.A.Victory. Conquest's full name is George Robert Acworth Conquest. Aha, I think we may say we have another pseudonym here. And Ted Pauker makes me think of Edward Pygge, a name used very generally by writers for *The New Statesman*, an English weekly journal of the left, affectionately known by aficionados as The Staggers, perhaps because it is always short of money. It was once, in happier days, well known for its back half—the literary pages, containing work by Martin Amis and Clive James, among others. Of course Ted Pauker is not (quite) Edward Pygge. Indeed, recourse to *Wikipedia* reveals it is indeed Robert Conquest again, a man of the right who wouldn't be seen dead within the pages of The Staggers. Ted Pauker writes limericks, the same limericks attributed to Jeff Chaucer. He also wrote limicks or limeaiku. Here is one of those.

> There's a vile old **man**
> Of Ja**pan** who **roars** at **whores**.
> "Where's your effing **fan**."

As you see it is a haiku which contains all the rhymes of a limerick. The sort of man who invents a form like that . . . is a very special sort of a man.

Kingsley Amis' *The New Oxford Book of Light Verse* contains two poems by Ted Pauker and several limericks by Victor Gray, all of which are also to be found in *A Garden of Erses*. I think we may hazard that all the (108) are Conquest's. This is The Book of Conquest's Limericks, all of them more or less rude, some of them *so* rude that I could not possibly quote them here. But rudery is often thought of as absolutely vital to the form, though I have to say here that I know of two Conquest Limericks, both among his very best, that you could recite to your Auntie. Here is my favorite, not, alas, to be found here.

> There was a great Marxist called Lenin
> Who did two or three million men in.
> That's a lot to have done in,
> But where he did one in,
> That grand Marxist Stalin did ten in.

You get more than the limericks here. You get a truncated version of Conquest's essay on The Limerick, reprinted from the *Times Literary Supplement*. It is also to be found in its fullest form in Conquest's book of Literary Essays *The Abomination of Moab*, well worth a look, even perhaps a purchase, if I may say so here, for other essays. I would single out the brilliant attempt (and failure) to translate two lines of Rimbaud, which says more, in little, than I have read anywhere else, about the impossibility, and yet the necessity of verse translation.

But we were talking of limericks. In his essay Conquest puts forward, then denies, the thesis that limericks are essentially "the folklore of the educated". Of course he is right that they are sung in rugby clubs and sergeants' messes—or at least they used to be. But it is still true that the ABSOLUTE NECESSITY for perfect scansion means that a book like this one, which *writes them down*, is a must. Oral transmission seems all too often to result in deterioration; the limerick no longer scans properly and the reciter either seems unaware of this, or worse, much worse, supposes that it doesn't matter. And, given the broken-backed, unrhythmical stuff that too often passes for poetry these days, I'm not at all surprised. So I suppose that the educated are complicit with the toiling masses here.

It has been suggested that the limerick is essentially an anecdote. Indeed Conquest quotes an essay in the *TLS* which claims that its structure is that of the Greek Tragedy. Now that I read the passage again I can't help wondering whether the essay, which Conquest cannot identify, ever existed outside his fertile imagination. And, as he says, not all limericks are stories, tragic or otherwise. The alternative qualities "are wit and fantasy".

Wit and fantasy are very much in evidence in one of my favorite Conquest limericks, which also demonstrates his predilection for double and treble rhymes. The Byron of *Don Juan* would have been proud to have written this one.

> Charlotte Brontë said, "Wow, sister! *What* a man!
> He laid me face down on the ottoman.
> Now don't you and Emily
> Go telling the femily,
> But he smacked me upon my bare bottom, Anne!"

I have restored Conquest's original spelling of "femily" because it makes the rhyme better and suggests that Charlotte had adopted an upmarket accent for her forays south from Haworth. Conquest is, when all is said and done, a literary man, and Dickens (five times), both Brownings, Keats, Landor, Leigh Hunt, Clough, Arnold, Swinburne, Blake, Jane Austen, Eliot, Pound, Byron and Shelley all make appearances. Edna St. Vincent Millay and Robert Frost appear in one of his masterpieces. Is it too crude to quote? Oh well, if you twist my arm.

> Said Edna St Vincent Millay,
> "At the poetry reading today
> They dragged Robert Frost off
> But not till he'd tossed off,
> And that was as good as a play."

You will see that it succeeds for an exactly opposite reason to the Brontë piece. We might suppose that in some parallel universe Charlotte really did get her bottom smacked and liked it (think Mr. Rochester), but there is nowhere that Robert Frost.... And that is partly what makes it funny. Frost and St. Vincent Millay are juxtaposed entirely because of rhyme. It could just as well have been Whitman and Emily Dickinson. Let me see, Whitman, Shit, man! Fit man . . . Dickinson. . . . Yes, ye-e-es.

Conquest is also, of course, a "serious" poet and last year he published *Penultimata*, which is a good book, as I said in a review in the Australian journal *Quadrant*. I also said that a collection of his limericks would be very welcome. And now you see. Well, I admit there were other people saying the same thing.

There must be room for one more limerick. I have chosen another not printed here. Perhaps it is only to be found in *The Abomination of Moab* for it was never printed in the *TLS*, for which august journal it was written.

> He was reading the Literary Supplement,
> When I asked what his, "Oh, stuff it up!" plea meant.
> He said, "Two lousy bits
> By prejudiced nits!"
> But they all are, so who knows which couple he meant?

That's the way to do it. Or at least I think so. And if you think so too, buy the book. I cannot believe you will regret it.

Catherine Chandler

Delineations

Wild geese flee the coming cold and ice,
    sketching the sky with epic Vs;
        no roundabout for these—
            their route precise.

Starlings in formation never jostle—
    aggregates of living art,
        together yet apart
            in graceful rustle.

Patterns of exuberant design,
    cadenza, cadence, wavelength, arrow,
        slant or straight and narrow—
            theirs, mine.

Catherine Chandler

Flammarion Woodcut Pilgrim Redux

He scans the sky and wonders if the Hubble
will burst (or not) the quintessential bubble,
plotting new data on a deep field chart
light years removed from any human heart.

Susan McLean

Moonburned

Stumbling on root-filled paths, I found my moon.
I trailed you like a begging hound, my moon.

A high wind swells your silver sail tonight.
Where is your heady cargo bound, my moon?

The jewels in my chest bed down on cotton.
Clouds and autumn mists confound my moon.

Shadows of hemlocks thrust like knives at my house.
Ice crystals dance in a ring around my moon.

My comforter, like a snowdrift, gives no comfort.
The ball of yarn on which I'm wound: my moon.

A screech owl shrieks; small darters freeze to listen.
Earth's cruelties do not astound my moon.

White-bereted fence posts glimmer in the dark.
Do you rest, like bulbs, beneath the ground, my moon?

A budding maple holds you in slender arms.
Her emptiness cannot surround my moon.

You float in every puddle, every window.
So close, so distant—who has drowned my moon?

I, Susan, sing this spell to draw you nearer.
Your spring-tide pull is so profound, my moon.

Richard Meyer

Communion

The moon's a sacramental host,
night air the eucharistic wine
for those who can't give up the ghost
of finding love incarnadine.

I take the moonlight on my tongue
and drink the linden-blossomed air,
remembering when I was young
and mouthed the same unanswered prayer.

John Slater

Falling Asleep

Sometimes even the monkey falls from the tree.
—Japanese proverb

Those zen monks sitting in all-day zazen,
face to the wall, eyes open just a bit
so as not to fall asleep; tough, brazen
almost in their diligence, they watch, sit.
It's said, on the edge of enlightenment,
Bodhidharma, alone in his cave
after long years of sitting in constant
watch, began to nod, drift . . . and to save
himself, sliced off his drooping eyelids.
Some zen monks in Japan, to keep awake,
will sit, calm as kamikaze pilots,
perched high up on a tree-top: which gave
rise to the saying of the Japanese,
Sometimes even monks fall from the trees.

Kim Bridgford

Billy Wilder's Grave

So there you are, with Lemmon on your left,
And mourners drifting through. They smile at what
Is written on your stone, and what is set
On Jack's. Yet Marilyn's the one the bereft

Come to see: extravagant and late,
Her skirt a lavish orchid gone adrift.
They bring mementoes, take a moment's seat,
To send their prayers, like silver clouds, aloft.

A connoisseur, you were meticulous
In art, in life, and in your movie patter.
It's not for crowds you wanted things to matter
(Although, of course, they helped, and made you famous).
No, it was for the writer who saw in your wit
That you took cinema, transcended it.

Diane Seuss

What's beneath the surface of the sonnet?

My favorite part of drag is taking it off.
—Divine

Below the pier, between the ribs of ships,
inside the boathouse, down the whale's throat . . .
the air between the dots in the ellipse,
the nothingness that rests inside the half note.
Let's slice our fear, expose its hollow core.
Let's halve a squash and scrape out all the seeds,
pull up linoleum, expose the rotten floor,
and pry up love until its fingers bleed.
The wedding gown conceals the naked girl,
her goose bumps draped across her skeleton.
Behind the rib cage built of shimmering pearl
and marrow, the heart lurks, soft as gelatin,
enfolded on itself, a question mark,
whispering its iambics in the dark.

FICTION

Marge Lurie
Heat Wave

For the past six days running, it had been 98 degrees in the shade. Though it was unusual weather for San Francisco, Carla had felt like she could handle it until the night before, when her air conditioner had given out. They were predicting another week of sweltering heat. She'd called every store within a fifty-mile radius. Not one had anything they'd be able to install until Monday. "Sorry, ma'am," she'd heard over and over again, until she thought she might scream.

Were Tim still around, he would have known how to rig something up to get the air conditioner working again, at least for a little while. He was handy that way.

Carla placed her order for a new unit and considered her options: spending the weekend with her sister Lizzie and her doctor-husband in Tiburon—she hated feeling like the poor relation; hopping a plane to somewhere and blowing all her savings—another non-option; or moving into her air-conditioned car for the weekend.

Though it was impossible to eat in weather like this, Carla took herself to the Midway Diner—midway between what and what she'd never known—and nursed a cup of coffee. Later, she ordered an egg salad plate, just to have a reason to keep sitting there. But eventually the waitress said she'd be needing the table for other customers, and cleared away the uneaten food.

Carla got back into her car and took Geary Boulevard out to the ocean. There, built into the rocks where the land met the sea, was the Musée Méchanique, a game room for tourists filled with miniature villages and mechanical toys from the Victorian era. And just by the entrance was Laughing Jack, a stubby mannequin dressed like a sailor. For a single quarter, he would laugh his sadistic laugh for what seemed like a good ten minutes. Just when you thought he was done, he would chortle one last time. Tim, the ex, had compared finding toys like Laughing Jack to getting lucky at a flea market. Today, in the sweltering heat, Jack's laugh seemed almost conspiratorial. Carla fed him twice, got back into her car, and let herself merge with the flow of traffic. It was just too hot to do anything else.

Everyone seemed to be heading north out of the city. Carla picked a car and decided to follow it. It was a gray Lexus. Once, when their Honda was in the repair shop, she and Tim had test-driven a Lexus. From the inside, it might have been a Mercedes. The dealer had encouraged them to lease it for the weekend. More and more couples were adopting new weekend lifestyles, he'd said. But they hadn't done more than given the Lexus a test-drive.

The gray Lexus Carla was following had local plates and the name of a dealership in Petaluma, a little ways north of the city. Carla couldn't make out much about its driver other than that he was middle-aged. His sunglasses made it impossible to see his eyes.

She put on her own sunglasses and trailed the man for twenty minutes, weaving gently in and out of lanes when he did, and over the Golden Gate Bridge, until suddenly the man pulled all the way from the far left lane to the far right, and signaled that he was turning off the freeway. For a moment, Carla thought she might lose him, but then the traffic opened up and they were heading north into the hills of Marin. They drove past Mill Valley into Larkspur. Though the grass alongside of the road was parched and dry like wheat now, the trees were still leafy and green. Winding up the narrow, blacktopped roads, Carla felt calmer and more purposeful. She rolled down her car window a hair to see if the heat had abated, discovered it hadn't, and rolled it back up again. She turned on her radio and there was Coltrane doing *A Love Supreme*.

Back when she and Tim were still in the Midwest, and Tim was teaching sculpture at the University in Bloomington, he played Coltrane for his students while they worked. She'd been one of his models then, but later she took the course for credit. And a year after that, when Tim was offered a position at the Art Institute in San Francisco, she went with him.

Despite the twists and turns in the single-lane road, it was easier to follow the Lexus here in the hills. Carla imagined that the man knew by now that she was following him. She'd gotten used to letting him make the decisions for both of them, and she imagined that he had as well. When he sped up, she sped up, and when he slowed down, she did too. It was almost as if they'd developed a rhythm. Then he surprised her.

His blinker went on, as if he were making a right turn into the next driveway. But he didn't make that right, or the next one, as if he'd thought better of it. The blinker went off and the man made two quick rights, and then pulled, without warning, into a long formal driveway. The horn beeped once and the man and his Lexus vanished behind a profusion of shrubs.

Carla drove on until she came to the next street sign, Redwood Drive, and pulled over to the curb. Why had the man beeped as he pulled into his driveway? Did he mistake her for a neighbor? Was he alerting someone that he was home? Did he have packages he needed help with?

Up a little ways, Carla noticed what looked to be a public tennis court. Two teenagers were just sliding their rackets into their cases. She drove up closer. Their shirts were sopping. Their temples and cheeks glistened. Their hair was matted with sweat. She watched the boys gather their belongings and disappear over the next hill.

Once they were out of sight, she pulled into the one parking spot beside the tennis court, collected her purse and sunglasses, and started back down the street. The house was invisible from the road. Nestled in the shrubs was a small security booth she hadn't noticed before. The booth was unmanned, so she let herself in. The lawn, a lush early summer green despite the heat, sloped gently toward a contemporary wood and glass house that seemed to have skylights everywhere. The sun glinted off the roof like diamonds.

Already the heat was like a wall pushing against her. It reminded her of her childhood. Sweltering Midwestern summers the only reward for winters that dragged on into May.

Carla heard them before she saw them—little sprinklers placed at perfect intervals all over the lawn. She slipped out of her sandals and pressed her feet, first one and then the other, up against one of the sprinklers, wiggling each toe and letting the water run down her soles before venturing further across the lawn.

She'd left her apartment, she now realized, without a thought as to what she was wearing. She hadn't planned on a house call. She was wearing the yellow sundress her sister had given her last year, when she and Tim split up. It was more something Lizzie would wear—a suburban frock—than anything Carla would pick out for herself. But she knew it became her.

Further down the lawn, she could see the Lexus parked in front of the house. Attached to the house were a carport and a three-car garage. They shimmered in the heat.

She tried to imagine the art that might deck the walls of this late 1970s home: a Larry Poons, a Richard Estes, maybe a Wayne Thiebaud to represent the West Coast. But no Klines or de Koonings, no Pollocks, no Rothkos.

The lawn was so plush it was almost like carpeting. She got down on her hands and knees and smelled the grass. She combed it with her fingers, and then when she'd found another sprinkler, she pressed her lips to it, as if she'd found water in a desert. She drank and drank from the thin stream until she was sated, and then she lay down to watch the sky.

The last time she'd been so brazen was at Lizzie's last spring. Lizzie and her husband had thrown a barbecue. She and Tim had gone, but he had spent the day ogling one of the servers. She couldn't have been more than seventeen. Perhaps he hadn't realized how obvious it was. To put it out of her mind, she'd let herself drink more than she would in an afternoon, and then she'd wandered off the patio onto the lawn. She lay down and pretended to make angels in the grass, as if it were a bed of snow. Later, she must have dozed, and when she came to, Tim was nudging her, telling her to gather her things, it was time to go. That was the last party she'd gone to.

Carla felt the man before she saw him. How could she have been so stupid? How had he walked right up to her—gotten so close—without her noticing? She sat upright.

"May I help you?" the man said. "You're not injured are you?"

"I'm so sorry. This isn't...." She rose to her feet. Reflexively, she combed her fingers through her hair. Her purse and sandals still lay on the lawn where she'd left them. "I must have dozed off for a moment. With this heat... I'm so sorry." She bent down quickly to pick up her belongings.

"You know on another day, a more temperate day, there would have been a guard at the front gate," the man said.

"Yes, of course. I saw the booth. I know. Forgive me."

The man said nothing. He appraised her slowly, carefully.

Carla endured it until his silence was too much. "You have a beautiful lawn," she said.

"Is that what drew you, then? My lawn?"

"It wasn't just that."

The man removed his sunglasses then. His eyes were the same steel-gray as his car. He looked mid-fortyish; ten years her senior. Fully grayed at the temples, salt and pepper everywhere else. But there wasn't any slackness yet around his jaw. He maintained himself well.

"Do you often follow people home?" the man continued. There was the tiniest line of perspiration above his lip. She could imagine him in an office, trying to close a deal, annoyed that it wasn't yet completed, but unflappable.

"You *were* following me, weren't you?"

Carla nodded. She felt naked without her sandals. She wondered if she could manage to put them on without upsetting him.

"Did you recognize me?"

"Why would I?"

"We've met before."

The man's face was immobile. Like a statue. Something Tim might have carved. And then he winked. The menace was there and then it was gone in the next instant.

Carla didn't say anything.

"You don't remember, do you?"

She shook her head, ever so slightly.

"Perhaps I'm confusing you with someone else." The man looked at his watch, swatted at the perspiration above his lip as if it were a mosquito. "Shall we sit on the patio, in the shade, and you can tell me what happened?"

"It's a simple explanation. I can tell you right here, and then I'll be gone."

"As you like." The man was well-dressed, not carelessly so like the richest rich. She'd seen his type at gallery openings.

"I didn't sleep at all last night. My air conditioner broke. You know, I haven't been myself. When I couldn't stand it any longer, I took myself for a drive."

"Sensible."

"Now you know," Carla said.

"But I don't. Not really. You haven't told me why you were following *me*."

"You seemed to know where you were going."

"Yes, I suppose I did."

"It was easier just to follow someone than to figure out where I was going. It was too hot to think." Carla dropped her sandals and slid her feet into them. They were soggy now. She could feel her toes clamming up. She wiggled them as inconspicuously as she could and turned toward the gate. "I should be going," she said. "I didn't mean to disturb you."

"But you aren't disturbing me. How rude of me. I haven't yet offered you anything to drink. Are you thirsty? I'm Walter, by the way." He extended his hand.

"Carla," she said extending hers.

The man turned away then, walked a yard or so, and then turned back. "I'll fix us something refreshing to drink. It won't take long. Please don't go. You like to swim, don't you?"

Carla nodded. "I'm a good swimmer."

"You looked like you might be. My wife was a good swimmer, too."

"Your wife?"

"Dead."

"I see."

"I put in the pool for her. Now I don't use it."

Walter headed once more toward the house. Carla watched him walk away. His stride was brisk. When he reached the door, she started back toward the gate. It was a long driveway. Would he come after her if she tried to get away? She felt in her bag for her cell phone. Would Tim care that she was in trouble now? They hadn't parted well. But still. She pulled the phone out. Once his number would have been programmed into it, but in their last conversation he'd told her he was moving across the Bay with his new girlfriend, another former student. Carla hadn't bothered to get the new number.

It was only after Tim had moved out that she had allowed herself to begin painting again. Landscapes from her childhood. Abstractions of color and shape that conjured the big open spaces of the Midwest. Spaces that had opened up inside of her once Tim was gone.

Carla wondered how Walter's wife had died. Had there been an accident? Or had she killed herself? Had he driven her to it with his impenetrability? Or perhaps done the job himself? And why had he mentioned the dead wife at all?

She wandered to the side of the house, looking for signs of life. A butler perhaps. Or a child. And then she saw it. The pool was set like a gem in a terraced lawn. She walked over to it. There were beds of wild anemones shooting up along a fence that marked where Walter's property ended. The coral and rose and purple blossoms rose up to different heights in a giddy display of color. Beyond them were the lemon trees.

Carla was admiring the garden when Walter reappeared. He'd changed out of his slacks and shirt into a bathing suit and silk robe. He had good, strong legs.

"There you are," he said. He took her arm and led her over to a beautiful glass table laid out with iced tea, cut lemons, and biscuits—all arrayed on a silver tray. Carla felt like she'd stumbled upon royalty. As she got closer, she saw the bathing suit Walter had picked out for her draped over one of the chairs.

"Home grown?" she asked, pointing to the lemon slices.

"Yes," Walter said.

"And this?" Carla nodded in the direction of the bathing suit.

"Store-bought." Walter took off his robe, dropped it on the chair beside the bathing suit. "You'll have a drink, a swim if you like, and then you can go back to your hot house with no air conditioning."

"How long has it been?" she asked.

"Five years. She—Elaine, that was her name—she died on her 33rd birthday. She was the age you are now. Am I right?"

Carla nodded again. "You've kept all her things?"

"I still have some of her things." Walter smiled his first smile, showing Carla his perfect teeth.

Carla took a sip of tea.

"You'll join me when you're ready." He walked over to the diving board, tested it for spring, and made a jack-knife dive. He swam the first length of the pool underwater and then when he'd reached the edge, he surfaced, smiled again, and swam another two laps. She'd known he would be a good swimmer.

When he returned to her side of the pool, he pulled himself halfway up out of the water. "There's a dressing room just to your left, on the other side of this wall. You can change in there," he said.

Carla took another sip of tea and picked up the bathing suit. It was a black one-piece. Her size. She started toward the dressing room and was almost there when she stopped herself.

"Should I tell you now?" he asked.

"Tell me?" The water was pooling around him.

"How we met?"

"You're so sure we have?" With his hair slicked back, he looked younger than before, almost like an athlete.

"It was at a party. Last spring. A lawn party in Tiburon. You were wearing a dress like the one you've got on now. But it was blue. I like this color on you better."

Carla pulled at the hem of her dress, as if she'd forgotten what she wearing.

"It becomes you."

She set the bathing suit back down on the chair.

"I can see I've upset you. I'm sorry."

Walter pulled himself up out of the pool and walked toward her. Why hadn't she left when it would still have been easy?

She took another sip of tea, and then set the cup down again. Once, back in Bloomington, she'd taken an art appreciation class that covered the decorative arts. The tea service looked like Meissen porcelain. Fussier than she liked, really. She imagined the wife had picked it out.

"It's not that," she said. "I remember the party. But I don't remember you."

"You seemed distracted."

"Maybe I was."

"But you're not distracted now?"

"Not anymore."

"Good. I'll swim a bit more, I think." Walter walked back to the diving board, and out to the edge. And then he turned himself around. This time he did a back flip into the water. She counted the seconds, waiting for him to reappear.

And when he did, she slipped Lizzie's yellow sundress over her head. She would not wear a dead woman's bathing suit. She paused for a moment and then peeled off her bra and underwear, too.

She remembered the first day she'd felt Tim's eyes on her. Boring into her. As if he were seeing parts of her that she herself couldn't see. She'd never shown her body to anyone before that day she modeled for his class. And suddenly there had been multiple pairs of eyes trained on her. She'd wanted to flee, but she'd forced herself to stay.

Walter held out his hand for her and helped her into the pool, and then they swam until they were too tired to swim anymore. Later, he'd shown her his house. She'd been wrong about the art. There wasn't a lot of it, but in the bedroom there was one small, gem-like field of flowers. A tiny Monet. The colors were lush like the anemones in Walter's garden.

Catharine Savage Brosman

On the Mesa Top

Here we are atop the vast, imposing mesa
called the "Monument"—a monument to nature, certainly.
It's really a huge canyon complex, cut out
by the ages through stone layers, notched and denticled,
with monoliths standing alone, tragic figures
left when other actors and some scenery were blown
away. Getting here takes time, on shelf roads,
serpentine and steep. But what a vista! Book Cliffs,

whitewashed in the light, stretch out northwest;
eastward, the Grand Mesa breaks, a massive tidal wave
unfurling into troughs and plains. We've found a table
for our lunch, within a circle of red cedar
and fine Utah juniper, with twisted trunks and berries, blue,
so plentiful that vats of gin could be produced
from just one tree. So, we get out cool water
and the leftovers from last night's dinner. The air

is dry, the blue as if distilled, the sunlight, brilliant
through dense whorls of leaves and louvered
limbs. Suddenly, a swishing sound, and fluttering: a bird
dives past my shoulder, drops, and settles
on the table edge before us. He's been here before;
he knows there's food, and dares to trust us. He's
a Colorado jay, just slightly crested, azure as a shadowy
distant mountain. His feet are delicate but long,

prehensile; the legs are tiny stilts. We stare, not moving,
watching him watch us. He wings off to a tree
just opposite, rejoins (we think) his mate, imparts
some matters. She also, then, swoops down
and lands, looking interrogative. When she in turn flies
back into the thicket, I take out a roll, part-eaten,
tear it, place the pieces where the birds'
sweet presence left a rustling after them. No further

invitation is required; here he is: a gust, a glide, a swerve,
and half the bread is carried off. Shortly,
she arrives and takes the rest. What ease, yet what
commotion as they gather in the weathered heart
of the juniper! It remains for us—birds in the wilderness
and kin—to feel their hidden being, celebrate
their passage, know this moment on the immemorial
rock, leaving behind no crumbs, but thoughts, thoughts.

Catharine Savage Brosman

Ars poetica

In art I like verisimilitude—
not slavish imitation of the real,
but—even the extraordinary—viewed
for truth's increase and durable appeal.

The murderer may be portrayed, the fraud,
though less than monstrous: thus Medusa's snakes
need combing; tragic figures we applaud
must not seem more perverse than their mistakes.

Peculiarities and accidents
of landscape, person, fruit need not be changed,
yet profit from restraint and ornaments.
The tulip's streaks may well be rearranged,

as language purged of oaths and vulgar words,
save bits of flavoring: a phrase or so
reveals the man; we do not want the turds.
Since verities depend on what we know

already, hid in shadows of neglect,
the artist's light should rarely be extreme,
nor must his lens distort—instead, direct
uncommon focus to a common theme,

by vision, measured understanding, tact.
Depict, then, golden peach and worm; eschew
grotesque or alien creature, vicious act;
use artifice to complement what's true.

AbleMUSE
A REVIEW OF POETRY, PROSE & ART

After more than a decade of online publishing excellence Able Muse begins a bold new chapter with its print edition

We continue to bring you in print the usual masterful craft with poetry, fiction, essays art & photography, and book reviews

Check out our 10+ years online archives for work by:

RACHEL HADAS • X.J. KENNEDY • TIMOTHY STEELE • MARK JARMAN • A.E. STALLINGS • DICK DAVIS • A.M. JUSTER • TIMOTHY MURPHY • DEBORAH WARREN • CHELSEA RATHBURN • RHINA P. ESPAILLAT • TURNER CASSITY • RICHARD MOORE • STEPHEN EDGAR • ANNIE FINCH • THAISA FRANK • NINA SCHUYLER • SOLITAIRE MILES • MISHA GORDIN • & SEVERAL OTHERS

SUBSCRIPTION

Able Muse - Print Edition - Subscriptions:

Able Muse is published semiannually.

Subscription rates for individuals: $22.00 per year; single and previous issues: $14.95.

International subscription rate: $29 per year; single and previous issues: $17.95.

Subscribe online at: **www.ablemusepress.com**

Or send a check payable to "Able Muse Review" to:
Attn: Alex Pepple - Editor, Able Muse, 467 Saratoga Avenue #602, San Jose, CA 95129 USA

COMING SOON
SPRING/SUMMER 2011
from
Able Muse Press

Nevertheless

POEMS
by Wendy Videlock

Lines of Flight

POEMS
by Catherine Chandler

www.AbleMusePress.com

Able Muse Write Prize
for poetry & fiction

» **$500 prize** *for the poetry winner, plus*

» **$500 prize** *for the fiction winner*

» *plus,* **publication** *in Able Muse (Print Edition)*

» **Blind judging** *by the final judges*

» *Final Judges*: Rachel Hadas (poetry); Alan Cheuse (fiction)

» *Entry Deadline:* February 15, 2011

**GUIDELINES & ENTRY INFORMATION
AVAILABLE ONLINE AT:**

www.ablemusepress.com

Able Muse Book Prize
for poetry

» **$1000 prize** *for winning manuscript, plus*

» *plus,* **publication** *by Able Muse Press*

» *All poetry styles welcome (metrical & free verse)*

» **Blind judging** *by the final judge*

» **Final Judge**: Andrew Hudgins

» **Entry Deadline:** March 31, 2011

**GUIDELINES & ENTRY INFORMATION
AVAILABLE ONLINE AT:**
www.ablemusepress.com

CONTRIBUTORS' NOTES

David Alpaugh has lived in California for 45 years but has yet to lose his New Jersey accent. His collection, *Counterpoint*, won the Nicholas Roerich Poetry Prize from Story Line Press. He has been a finalist for Poet Laureate of California. His poems have appeared in *Evergreen Review, The Formalist, The Hypertexts, Light, Raintown Review, Poetry,* and many other journals. His controversial essays on "po-biz" can be read online at *Houston Poetry Review, Mudlark, Rattle,* and *The Chronicle of Higher Education.*

Peter Austin lives with his wife and three daughters in Toronto, where he teaches English at Seneca College. He is a New Formalist poet. Over 200 of his poems have appeared in magazines/anthologies in the USA, Canada, the UK, Germany, South Africa, Australia, Israel and New Zealand. As well as poetry, he writes plays, and his musical adaptation of *The Wind in the Willows* has been produced four times, most recently in Worcester, Massachusetts. His first collection of poems, *A Many-Splendored Thing*, was published in July 2010.

Ned Balbo's latest book is *The Trials of Edgar Poe and Other Poems* (Story Line Press/WCU Poetry Center), selected for the 2010 Donald Justice Prize by A.E. Stallings. His previous books are *Lives of the Sleepers* (U. of Notre Dame Press, Ernest Sandeen Prize and *ForeWord* Book of the Year), and *Galileo's Banquet* (Towson University Prize). He has also published a chapbook, *Something Must Happen* (Finishing Line Press) and has poems out or forthcoming in *The Hopkins Review, Sewanee Theological Review, River Styx,* and elsewhere.

John Beaton was raised in the Highlands of Scotland and lives on an acreage in Qualicum Beach on Vancouver Island, Canada. An actuary by profession, he is now retired from a career in the pensions industry. He and his wife have raised five children. For almost 4 years, he was a moderator of The Deep End workshop at *Eratosphere*. His poetry has been widely published in literary and non-literary newspapers, magazines, journals, and anthologies, and has won poetry competitions. He is a regular spoken-word performer at Celtic events, Burns Suppers, and literary gatherings.

Kim Bridgford is the director of the West Chester University Poetry Center and the West Chester University Poetry Conference. As editor of *Mezzo Cammin*, she was the founder of The *Mezzo Cammin* Women Poets Timeline Project, which was launched at the National Museum of Women in the Arts in Washington on March 27, 2010, and will eventually be the largest database of women poets in the world. Her new book is *Take-Out: Sonnets about Fortune Cookies* (David Robert Books).

Catharine Savage Brosman, who now lives in Houston, is Professor Emerita of French at Tulane University. She spent her girlhood in Colorado and West Texas and graduated from Rice University. In addition to numerous works on French literary history, she has published seven collections of verse and four chapbooks. *Range of Light* (LSU Press, 2007), which includes many southwestern landscape poems, and *Breakwater* (Mercer University Press, 2009) received starred reviews in *Booklist*. Two new collections are forthcoming: *Under the Pergola* (2011) and *On the North Slope* (2012). Her poems have appeared widely, in such journals as *Sewanee Review*, *Southern Review*, *Critical Quarterly*, and *Southwest Review*. French translations of her poems have appeared in the *Nouvelle Revue Française* and *Europe*.

Steve Bucknell is a poet and Mental Health Nurse working in Sheffield. He has published poems and reviews in magazines such as *The Wide Skirt, Staple, Pennine Platform, Poetry Nottingham* and others.

Nancy Lou Canyon holds the MFA in Creative Writing from Pacific Lutheran University and a Certificate in Fiction Writing from University of Washington. Her prose and poetry is published in *Water~Stone Review, Fourth Genre, Floating Bridge Review, Poetry South, Main Street Rag, Exhibition, Obliquity,* and more. She is a Fiction Editor for *Crab Creek Review*, as well as a creative writing instructor for Whatcom Community College and Western Washington University's Academy of Life Long Learning. Her current writing project is the revision of a memoir about divorce. She and her Tuxedo cat named Sid live in historic Fairhaven, along the shore of Bellingham Bay in the Pacific Northwest.

Catherine Chandler, an American poet born in New York City and raised in Pennsylvania, completed her graduate studies at McGill University in Montreal where she has lectured in the Department of Languages and Translation for many years. Her poems, interviews, essays and English translations from French and Spanish have been published in numerous print and online journals and anthologies in the United States, the United Kingdom, Canada and Australia. She is co-editor of *Passages* (The Greenwood Centre for Living History), and author of two chapbooks, *For No Good Reason* and *All or Nothing*. Her first full-length poetry collection, *Lines of Flight*, will be published by Able Muse Press in the spring/summer of 2011.

Stephen Collington studied English and Chinese at the University of Toronto, and Comparative Literature at the University of Tokyo. Which is as much as to say, writing in English about writing Chinese poetry in Japanese is the sort of thing that almost comes naturally to him at this point. (He also writes some poems himself now and then, though not always in Chinese.) He would like to dedicate his article to Naomi Fukumori, fellow student and friend, with thanks for the improbable gift of *The Anyone-Can-Do-It Method* all those years ago.

Kevin Corbett, the oldest of five, grew up in west Michigan. He graduated from Grand Valley State University in Allendale, Michigan with a degree in English Secondary Education. Currently, he lives in the Metro Detroit area where he works as a substitute teacher. His poetry has appeared or will appear in *14 by 14* and *The Lavender Review*.

Maryann Corbett is the author of two chapbooks, *Dissonance* (Scienter Press, 2009) and *Gardening in a Time of War* (Pudding House, 2007). She is a past winner of the Willis Barnstone Translation Prize and the Lyric Memorial Award and a finalist for the Morton Marr prize. Her poems, essays, and translations have appeared in more than sixty journals in print and online, including *River Styx, Atlanta Review, The Evansville Review,* and *The Dark Horse,* as well as *The Able Muse Anthology* and *Hot Sonnets,* forthcoming from Entasis Press. She lives in St. Paul and works for the Minnesota Legislature.

Emily Cutler is a junior at Indian Springs School. She has published her writings in *Chicken Soup for the Soul: Teens Talk Middle School, Aura Literary Arts Review, Cicada Magazine, Polyphony H.S.,* and *New Moon Magazine,* and her writings are upcoming in *The Minetta Review* and on *Every Day Poets* online. Besides writing, she enjoys helping teach English as a Second Language and playing the piano.

Trina L. Drotar, a San Francisco native currently residing in Sacramento, comes to poetry through prose, art, music, and design. She is working on a collection of prose and poetry, *Night Garden*, for her MA thesis. She is the current editor of *Poetry Now* and former editor of *Calaveras Station*. Her work has appeared on *Medusa's Kitchen* and *Ophidian*, and in *WTF, Word Riot, Rattle,* and *Brevities*.

Peter Filkins is the author of three books of poetry, most recently *Augustine's Vision*. He has also translated the poetry and prose of Ingeborg Bachmann, and the novels of H.G. Adler. A new Adler novel, *Panorama*, will appear this January from Random House. He is the recipient of a Berlin Prize, the Stover Award in Poetry, and fellowships at Yaddo, MacDowell, and the Millay Colony, and his work has appeared in numerous journals, including *The New Criterion, Sewanee Review, Narrative,* and *The Iowa Review*. He teaches writing and literature at Bard College.

Rebecca Foust's book, *All That Gorgeous, Pitiless Song,* won the Many Mountains Moving Book Prize and was released in April 2010. Also released in 2010 was *God, Seed* (Tebot Bach Press), environmental poetry with art by Lorna Stevens. Two chapbooks, *Mom's Canoe* and *Dark Card,* received the Robert Phillips Poetry Chapbook Prizes in 2007 and 2008.

Jamie Iredell is the author of *Prose. Poems. A Novel.* (Orange Alert Press, 2009), and of *The Book of Freaks* (Future Tense Books, 2011). He lives in Atlanta.

J. Patrick Lewis' first book of poems, *Gulls Hold Up the Sky*, was just published by Laughing Fire Press. His poems have appeared in *Gettysburg Review, New Letters, Southern Humanities Review, new renaissance, Fine Madness, Light Quarterly,* and many others. He has also published 65 children's poetry and picture books to date with Knopf, Atheneum, Dial, Harcourt, Little, Brown, National Geographic, Creative Editions, Chronicle Books, Scholastic, Candlewick, and others.

R.P. Lister — see page 81.

Marge Lurie's fiction has appeared in *Ep;phany: A Literary Journal*, *Able Muse Anthology*, and online at *Pindeldyboz.com*, *Ablemuse.com*, *Ducts.org*, *Fictionwarehouse.com*, and *onelastcarcrash.net*. She earned her M.F.A. from the New School and has also studied at The Writers Studio in New York and the Fine Arts Work Center in Provincetown, Massachusetts. She lives in New York City.

Ted Mc Carthy was born in Clones, Ireland, where he currently lives and works as a teacher. His work has appeared in magazines in Ireland, the UK, Europe, Australia and the US, and has won a number of awards, including the Brendan Behan Award for best debut collection for *November Wedding*. An annual associate of the Flat Lake Festival, Ireland, he has written a number of one-act plays, and is currently involved in writing and developing scripts for short films, as well as judging film festival shorts.

Susan McLean, an English professor at Southwest Minnesota State University, won the 2009 Richard Wilbur Award for her first poetry book, *The Best Disguise*. Her poems and translations from Latin and French have appeared in *Measure*, *The Classical Outlook*, *The Raintown Review*, and elsewhere.

Richard Meyer, now retired from the classroom, taught high school English and humanities for thirty-two years. He lives in his family home, the house his father built, in Mankato, a city at the bend of the Minnesota River.

Leslie Monsour's most recent book is *The Alarming Beauty of the Sky* (Red Hen Press). In 2007 she received a Fellowship in Literature from the National Endowment for the Arts. She lives in Los Angeles, California, where she writes, teaches, edits, and sings.

Frank Osen lives in Pasadena, California, where, after a career as corporate general counsel and real estate investor, he's found a place in the Old Reference Room of the Huntington Library, as the Old Reference Librarian. His work has recently appeared or is forthcoming in *The Raintown Review*, *The Spectator (UK)*, *The Dark Horse*, *The Flea*, *Snakeskin*, *32 Poems*, and the *Evansville Review*. He won the 2008 Best American Poetry series poem award, was first runner-up in 2008 Morton Marr competition, a finalist in the 2006 Howard Nemerov sonnet competition, and placed fourth in the 2010 Writers Digest competition.

Gilbert Wesley Purdy's work in poetry, prose and translation has appeared in many fine journals, paper and electronic, including: *Jacket Magazine*, *Poetry International*, *The Georgia Review*, *Grand Street*, *The Evansville Review*, *SLANT*, *Orbis*, *Consciousness Literature and the Arts*, and *Quarterly Literary Review Singapore*. He is the regular reviewer of volumes of poetry and poetry-related prose for the online journal *Eclectica*.

Massimo Sbreni — see page 49.

Diane Seuss is Writer in Residence at Kalamazoo College in Michigan. Her most recent collection, *Wolf Lake, White Gown Blown Open*, won the 2009 Juniper Prize for Poetry from the University of Massachusetts Press. It was published in April 2010. New work has appeared in *Poetry*, *The Georgia Review*, *New Orleans Review*, and *Brevity*.

John Slater is a Cistercian monk in upstate New York where he cares for the sick and tends a quasi-Japanese garden. His poems and translations have appeared in various journals including *PN Review*, *Canadian Literature* and *Crab Orchard Review*. *The Tangled Braid: Ninety-Nine Poems by Hafiz of Shiraz*, which he co-translated with Jeffrey Einboden, was recently published by Fons Vitae. *Surpassing Pleasure*, a first collection of his own work, will appear in the Spring of 2011 from The Porcupine's Quill.

Julie Stoner is a longtime participant of *Able Muse*'s online poetry forum, *Eratosphere*. A finalist for the 2009 Howard Nemerov Sonnet Award, she is even prouder of her role in the international effort toward posthumous publication of M.A. Griffiths' collected works (forthcoming in 2011 from Arrowhead Press). She lives in San Diego, California.

Marilyn L. Taylor is currently serving as the Poet Laureate of the state of Wisconsin. She taught for many years at the University of Wisconsin-Milwaukee for the Department of English and for the university's Honors College, and has also served as visiting poet at many other institutions both within Wisconsin and throughout the country. The most recent of her six collections of poetry, titled *Going Wrong*, was published by Parallel Press in 2009. Taylor's award-winning poems have appeared in many anthologies and journals, including *The American Scholar*, *Poetry*, *Smartish Pace*, *Measure*, *Able Muse*, and *Mezzo Cammin*. She is a Contributing Editor for *The Writer* magazine, where her columns on poetic craft appear bi-monthly.

Catherine Tufariello's first poetry collection, *Keeping My Name* (Texas Tech, 2004), was a finalist for the 2005 Los Angeles Times Book Prize and winner of the 2006 Poets' Prize. Her poems have appeared widely in journals and have been anthologized in *The Seagull Reader*, *Western Wind*, *The New Penguin Book of Love Poetry*, and elsewhere. A native of Buffalo, New York, Catherine lives with her husband and daughter in Valparaiso, Indiana, where she is a staff member of the Project on Civic Reflection at Valparaiso University.

Wendy Videlock's book, *Nevertheless*, is due out from Able Muse Press in the spring/summer of 2011.

Gail White is the author of *The Accidental Cynic*, a winner of the Anita Dorn Memorial Award for Poetry, and *Easy Marks*, a nominee for the Poets Prize. She is also the subject of Julie Kane's essay "Getting Serious About Gail White's Light Verse", which appeared in *Mezzo Cammin*. She lives in Breaux Bridge, Louisiana, with her husband and cats, and reads obsessively, especially Victorian novels.

John Whitworth is one of those fattish, baldish, backward-looking, provincial poets in which England is so rich (perhaps *too* rich). His ninth collection, *Being the Bad Guy*, was published by Peterloo in November 2007. Les Murray likes it. Good on him. You might also consider *Writing Poetry* published by A & C Black, one of those how-to books; it has run to a second edition and is pretty good, though he (the poet) would say that, wouldn't he?

Steven Winn's work has appeared in *Alaska Quarterly Review*, *Cimarron Review*, *Colorado Review*, *Florida Review*, *Prairie Schooner*, *Southern Poetry Review*, *ZYZZYVA* and elsewhere. He is a former Wallace Stegner Fellow at Stanford University and spent 28 years as a critic of arts and culture at the *San Francisco Chronicle*.

Heather Hallberg Yanda teaches in the English Department at Alfred University in the hills of upstate New York. Her poems have been published or are forthcoming in *Sojourners*, *The White Pelican Review*, and *The Yale Journal of Medical Humanities* among others. Her first collection of poems, *The Neighbors' Beautiful Daughters*, is currently looking for a publisher.

ACKNOWLEDGEMENTS

"Heat Wave" appeared briefly online at *FOTE*

Cover image by Massimo Sbreni

Cover & book design by Alexander Pepple

Grateful acknowledgment of our proofreaders extraordinaires: Gregory Dowling, Janice D. Soderling and Julie Stoner

INDEX

A

"A Cautionary Tale" 34
"A Crisis in Mesa Verde" 94
After the Revival 119
A Garden of Erses: Limericks,
    Introduced by Robert Conquest 130
Alpaugh, David 47, 155
"A Photographic Exhibit" 49
"Ars poetica" 150
Art & Photography 49
"A Terrible Storm" 1
"At the Hotel Ukrainya - A Century Ago" 96
Austin, Peter 4, 155

B

Balbo, Ned 102, 155
Beaton, John 104, 155
"Billy Wilder's Grave" 139
Book Reviews 119, 130
Bridgford, Kim 139, 155
Brosman, Catharine Savage 148, 150, 156
Bucknell, Steve 70, 81, 156

C

Canyon, Nancy Lou 1, 156
Chandler, Catherine 134, 135, 156
Chaucer, Jeff - *A Garden of Erses: Limericks*,
    Introduced by Robert Conquest 130
Collington, Stephen 16, 156
"Communion" 137
Corbett, Kevin 107, 156
Corbett, Maryann 34, 157
Cutler, Emily 108, 157

D

"Darling Death" 86

"Dear Moon," 100
"Debrief" 98
"Delineations" 134
Drotar, Trina L. 5, 157

E

Essays 6, 16, 36, 70

F

"Falling Asleep" 138
Featured Artist 49
Featured Poet 70, 81, 85
Featured Poetry 70, 81, 85, 86, 87, 88, 89, 90, 91,
    92, 93
Fiction 1, 108, 141
Filkins, Peter 6, 157
"Flammarion Woodcut Pilgrim Redux" 135
Foust, Rebecca 46, 156

H

"Heat Wave" 141
"His Own" 4

I

"In Beth's Garden" 101
"Infected Eyes" 88
"In My Pocket" 5
"In Such a Place" 103
Interviewed by Steve Bucknell 81
Interviews 49, 81
Iredell, Jamie 33, 157
"It Will Never Be Beautiful" 3

J

Jerrell, Carrie - *After the Revival* 119

K

Kumin, Maxine - *Where I Live: New & Selected Poems 1990-2010* 119

L

Lewis, J. Patrick 96, 157
"Ligan" 97
Lister, R.P. (Richard Percival) 70, 81, 85, 86, 87, 88, 89, 90, 91, 92, 93, 157
Lurie, Marge 141, 157

M

"Marco Polo Collects Bird Eggs" 102
Mc Carthy, Ted 45, 158
McLean, Susan 136, 158
Memoirs 70
Meyer, Richard 137, 158
Monsour, Leslie 103, 158
"Moonburned" 136

N

"Nature" 107
"Nearly" 45
"Nokia" 92

O

"On the Mesa Top" 148
Osen, Frank 97, 158

P

Poetry 3, 4, 5, 32, 33, 34, 44, 45, 46, 47, 70, 85, 86, 87, 88, 89, 90, 91, 92, 93, 94, 96, 97, 98, 100, 101, 102, 103, 104, 106, 107, 134, 135, 136, 137, 138, 139, 140, 148, 150
"*Postres*" 44
Purdy, Gilbert Wesley 32, 158

R

"Relativity" 108
"Richard Cory (His Untold Story)" 47

S

Sbreni, Massimo 49, 158
"Semi-Formal Verse and Its Prosody" 36
Seuss, Diane 140, 159
Slater, John 138, 159
"Stardust" 89
Stoner, Julie 119, 159

T

Taylor, Marilyn L. 36, 159
"The Anyone-Can-Do-It Method for Writing Chinese Poetry (in Japanese): Thoughts on Language, Authenticity and Form" 16
"The Cricket in the Sump" 106
"The Haunted" 87
"The Length of Time" 85
"The Mystery of R.P. Lister" 70
"The 'Other' Muse" 6
"The Quonset Hut" 32
"The Slot Tech" 33
"The Slow Loris" 90
"The Speaker Tries Medication" 46
"The Stork" 91
"To Be Alive" 93
"To the Dead of Winter" 104
Tufariello, Catherine 106, 159

V

Videlock, Wendy 98, 100, 101, 159

W

"What's beneath the surface of the sonnet?" 140
Where I Live: New & Selected Poems 1990-2010 119
White, Gail 94, 159
Whitworth, John 130, 160
Winn, Steven 44, 160

Y

Yanda, Heather Hallberg 3, 160

Able Muse Anthology

978-0-9865338-0-8 • $16.95

Edited by Alexander Pepple • *Foreword by* Timothy Steele

PRAISE FOR THE *ABLE MUSE ANTHOLOGY*:

This book fills an important gap in understanding what is really happening in early twenty-first century American poetry. **–Dana Gioia**

You hold in your hands a remarkable anthology of poems, translations, an interview, essays, short stories and visual art. **–David Mason**

This extraordinarily rich collection of fiction, poetry, essays and art by so many gifted enablers of the Muse is both a present satisfaction and a promise of future performance. **–Charles Martin**

Neither unskilled, lethargic, nor distracted from their proper enterprise, the muses in the past decade have been singularly able, as this outstanding anthology from *Able Muse* demonstrates. **–Catharine Savage-Brosman**

Here's a generous serving of the cream of *Able Muse*, including not only formal verse but nonmetrical work that also displays careful craft, memorable fiction (seven remarkable stories), striking artwork and photography, and incisive critical prose. **–X. J. Kennedy**

Mark Jarman, Rachel Hadas, Turner Cassity, Stephen Edgar, Timothy Steele, R. S. Gwynn, Rhina P. Espaillat, A. M. Juster, Geoffrey Brock, Annie Finch, X. J. Kennedy, Timothy Murphy, Jennifer Reeser, Beth Houston, Dick Davis, A. E. Stallings, Richard Moore, Chelsea Rathburn, David Stephenson, Julie Kane, Alan Sullivan, Kim Bridgford, Deborah Warren, Diane Thiel, Richard Wakefield, Rose Kelleher, Leslie Monsour, Lyn Lifshin, Amit Majmudar, Len Krisak, Marilyn L. Taylor, Dolores Hayden, Suzanne J. Doyle, Dennis Must, Thaisa Frank, Nina Schuyler, Misha Gordin, Solitaire Miles, and others.

from **Able Muse Press**

More information at: **www.ablemusepress.com**
Order at: **Amazon.com, BN.com, ...**
& other popular online & offline bookstores

www.ingramcontent.com/pod-product-compliance
Lightning Source LLC
Chambersburg PA
CBHW081917180426
43199CB00036B/2772